India-ASEAN Engagements

Economic and Social Dimensions

India-ASEAN Engagements

Economic and Social Dimensions

Edited by

Faisal Ahmed
Associate Professor and
Chairman of International Business Area,
FORE School of Management, New Delhi, India

and

Mohd. Faheem
Lecturer, Indian Studies Programme,
Pridi Banomyong International College,
Thammasat University, Bangkok, Thailand

New Century Publications
New Delhi, India

NEW CENTURY PUBLICATIONS
4800 / 24, Bharat Ram Road,
Ansari Road, Daryaganj,
New Delhi - 110 002 (India)

Tel.: 011-2324 7798, 4358 7398, 4101 7798

E-mail: info@newcenturypublications.com

www.newcenturypublications.com

Editorial office:
LG – 7, Aakarshan Bhawan,
4754-57/23, Ansari Road, Daryaganj,
New Delhi – 110 002

Tel.: 011-4356 0919

First Published: **2019**

ISBN: **978-81-7708-482-5**

Published by New Century Publications and printed at Milan Enterprises, New Delhi.

Designs: Patch Creative Unit, New Delhi.

PRINTED IN INDIA

About the Book

Association of Southeast Asian Nations (ASEAN) is an economically progressive, culturally vibrant and a geo-politically strategic congregation. It has a membership of 10 countries, namely Brunei Darussalam, Cambodia, Indonesia, Laos, Malaysia, Myanmar, Philippines, Singapore, Thailand and Vietnam.

India's engagement with ASEAN started with its *Look East Policy*. India became a Sectoral Dialogue Partner of ASEAN in 1992 and Full Dialogue Partner in 1996. In November 2001, ASEAN-India relationship was upgraded to the summit level.

India's engagement with ASEAN has been historically evolving as it shares strong civilizational and cultural ties with the countries of the region. Presently, India and ASEAN engage in economic, cultural and strategic spheres through the framework of *Act East Policy*.

The present volume contains 8 research articles which provide deep insights into India-ASEAN relations. Authored by experts in the field, these contributions add to the existing body of knowledge and discourse on economic, trade and cultural aspects of India-ASEAN engagements. The book focuses on contemporary and pragmatic discourses on the theme and would be useful for all those interested in understanding various facets of India-ASEAN co-operation.

About the Editors

Dr. Faisal Ahmed is Associate Professor and Chairman of International Business Area at FORE School of Management, New Delhi. His research and consulting areas include Indo-Pacific trade and geo-politics, economic integration, WTO issues, and south-south co-operation. He holds Masters and Doctoral degrees from India and Executive Certification in geo-political analysis from Geneva, Switzerland. He held the position of consultant to the United Nations Economic and Social Commission for Western Asia (UNESCWA). He has headed research projects supported by the Ministry of Commerce and Industry, and Ministry of External Affairs, Government of India. He is a member of International Political Science Association (IPSA), Montreal, Canada. His research papers have been published in national and international refereed journals indexed in scholarly databases of Scopus and Thomson-Clarivate.

Dr. Ahmed's articles have appeared in leading newspapers including *Financial Express*, *Bangkok Post*, *Business Standard*, *South China Morning Post* (Hong Kong), *Santiago Times* (Chile), and *The Straits Times* (Singapore). He has also been on expert panel of national and international TV channels.

Dr. Mohd. Faheem is currently lecturer in the Indian Studies Programme, Pridi Banomyong International College, Thammasat University, Bangkok, Thailand. He holds Masters and Ph.D. degrees from Aligarh Muslim University (AMU), Aligarh. He has published several articles in academically reputed journals and presented papers at various conferences/seminars. His areas of research interest include ASEAN, international migration and economic geography.

Contents

Contributors

Dedi Dinarto: Dedi Dinarto is a researcher at ASEAN Studies Centre, Faculty of Social and Political Sciences, Universitas Gadjah Mada, Indonesia. He is pursuing Masters Degree in International Relations at S. Rajaratnam School of International Studies. He has published several works in reputed media, including *The Jakarta Post, The Diplomat, Channel News Asia,* and *The Conversation.* His research areas include Indonesia's foreign policy, maritime security, politics and Riau Archipelago.

Maya Dania: Maya Dania is a Lecturer at School of Social Innovation, Mae Fah Luang University, Thailand. She holds Bachelor of Philosophy from Gadjah Mada University in Indonesia and M.A. in Southeast Asian Studies from Chulalongkorn University in Thailand. She has contributed several research articles in academic journals of repute. She was a fellow at National University of Singapore in 2015 and Malaya University in 2016.

Rajan Sudesh Ratna: Rajan Sudesh Ratna is working as Economic Affairs Officer, United Nations ESCAP Sub-Regional Office for South and South-West in New Delhi. His current assignment relates to providing support to the APTA secretariat, carry out research and analysis on international trade policy issues, especially those relating to the WTO and RTAs. Prior to joining UNESCAP, he had worked with the Government of India for 25 years, initially in the Directorate General of Foreign Trade and later in the Ministry of Commerce handling the regional and multilateral trade policy issues. He had also worked as Professor, Centre for WTO Studies, Indian Institute of Foreign Trade, New Delhi. He holds Ph.D. degree in Economics from the Indian Institute of Foreign Trade, New Delhi.

Jing Huang: Jing Huang is consultant in the FAO Regional Office for Asia and the Pacific. Her main work area is agriculture trade, food security and nutrition, as well as statistical analysis. Prior to joining FAO, she had worked with United Nations ESCAP, Bangkok. She has contributed to developing the APTA database on tariff concessions, non-tariff measures (NTMs) and rules of origin for the Fourth Round of APTA concessions. Her research interests include international trade, food security and nutrition, climate change and services trade liberalization. She has completed Ph.D. programme at Kyung Hee University's International Trade and Business School in Seoul, South Korea.

Reni Juwitasari: Reni Juwitasari is lecturer at School of Liberal Arts, Mae Fah Luang University, Thailand. She holds Masters Degree in Educational Administration from Mahasarakham University, Thailand. She has published a number of articles on education, especially leadership based on gender. Currently, she is conducting research on Japanese Occupation influence on education system in Indonesia.

Mohd. Faheem: Mohd. Faheem is currently Lecturer at the Indian Studies Programme, Pridi Banomyong International College, Thammasat University, Thailand. He holds Masters and Ph.D. degrees from Aligarh Muslim University, India. He worked for 3 years as visiting research fellow at the Institute of Asian Studies, Chulalongkorn University, Thailand. He has published several articles in journals and presented papers at various conferences and seminars.

A.N. Sarkar: A.N. Sarkar obtained his doctorate degree in Biochemistry from the University of Wales. He served the Indian Council of Agricultural Research and various Ministries of the Government of India as a scientist for 30 years. He worked as a chair Professor NABARD and as a Professor at University of Petroleum and Energy Studies. He was also Professor and Dean (Research) at Asia-Pacific Institute of Management, New Delhi. He has authored 6 books and published 100 research articles in reputed national and international journals.

M. Absar Alam: M. Absar Alam is Assistant Professor (Economics) with MKS College, LNM University, Darbhanga. He has worked as a consultant with Asian Development Bank (ADB), focussing on regional cooperation and transport facilitation. He has also worked as Senior Fellow with Asian Institute of Transport Development (AITD). He has published several research papers and articles in the field of transport economics and regional cooperation. His research and consulting areas include regional cooperation, transport facilitation, international trade theory and practices.

Sarfaraaj Nasir: Sarfaraaj Nasir is Associate Editor with *The Policy Times*. He has wide range of experience in the field of media, academics and research. Earlier, he was guest faculty at Jamia Millia Islamia, New Delhi and taught 'Incredible India' campaign, heritage and cultural tourism at both graduate and post-graduate levels. He specializes in history, journalism and tourism. He has also worked with All India Radio as an editor. He was also associated with AC Nielsen (a research organization) where he worked on a World Bank project 'Moving out of Poverty' (MoP).

Faisal Ahmed: Faisal Ahmed is Associate Professor and Chairman of International Business Area at FORE School of Management, New Delhi. His research and consulting areas include Indo-Pacific trade and geopolitics, economic integration, WTO issues, and south-south cooperation. He holds Masters and doctoral degrees from India and Executive Certification in geopolitical analysis from Geneva, Switzerland. He held the position of Consultant to the United Nations Economic and Social Commission for Western Asia (UNESCWA). He has led research projects supported by the Ministry of Commerce and Industry, and Ministry of External Affairs, Government of India. He is a member of International Political Science Association (IPSA), Montreal, Canada. His research papers have been published in national and international refereed journals indexed in scholarly databases of Scopus and Thomson-Clarivate.

Farhan Alam: Farhan Alam is Research Associate at FORE School of Management, New Delhi. He is presently working in a project on SIDS countries of the Indo-Pacific. He holds a Bachelor's degree in Geography and Master's degree, both from AMU, Aligarh. He has worked as consultant and researcher on refugees and livelihoods issues on projects supported by the United Nations High Commission for Refugees (UNHCR) in New Delhi. His research interests include climate change, refugee and migration studies, and sustainable livelihood.

Introduction

The Association of Southeast Asian Nations (ASEAN) was formed in 1967. Since its establishment it has evolved into a robust trade agreement. Today, the congregation can be referred to as an economically progressive, culturally vibrant and a geo-politically strategic one which has also gained centrality in Indo-Pacific discourse. From the historical trade routes to the Asian Financial Crisis, and from Mekong-Ganga Co-operation to mega-blocs like Regional Comprehensive Economic Partnership (RCEP) and Comprehensive and Progressive Trans-Pacific Partnership (CP-TPP), the region has fully or partially witnessed it all. ASEAN region is, in fact, socio-culturally quite rich, and this is evident from the narratives and discourses on education, culture or society in these countries. The region, therefore, has immense economic and cultural significance.

India's engagement with ASEAN has been historically evolving. India shares strong civilization and cultural ties with the countries of the region. Moreover, the trade and diplomatic relations between India and ASEAN countries are also witnessing an evolving trend. India and ASEAN have been engaging through the vision laid out by the 'Look East Policy' and the now the 'Act East Policy', and also through the frameworks of India-ASEAN FTA in Goods (2009) and India-ASEAN FTA in Services (2014). In fact, India and ASEAN are mutually indispensable for each other in terms of resources, sea routes, security, potential markets, investments, global value chains, cultural co-operation and connectivity.

The present edited volume thus brings together a set of 8 papers based on research work carried out by the respective authors from various ASEAN countries and India.

Dedi Dinarto in his paper *India's Act East Policy through Blue Economy Co-operation* focuses on India's relationship with Indonesia and assesses the prospects and challenges of co-operation between India and Indonesia on the issue of *blue economy*. The paper argues that India should invigorate its bilateral relationship with Indonesia through the blue economy co-operation if it is to strengthen its 'Act East Policy'.

Maya Dania in her paper *Women's Rights in India and Indonesia* makes a comparison of women's rights in India and Indonesia and argues that the issue of human rights for women cannot be separated from the discourse of violation against women.

Rajan Sudesh Ratna and Jing Huang in their paper *ASEAN-India Free Trade Agreement: Reducing Non-tariff Trade Cost* use the gravity model of trade to evaluate the impact of elimination of non-tariff related trade costs on AIFTA exports keeping in view the future negotiating prospects. The paper finds that NTMs are becoming much stronger determining factors in bilateral trade than the traditional tariff barrier measures which could provide restricted market access.

Reni Juwitasari in her paper titled *Education System in ASEAN and South Asia Region: A Comparison* compares the system in ASEAN and South Asia with specific reference to gender-based education in Indonesia and India. She argues that education plays a role to empower people, especially girls, to elevate better life, though it needs to break gender stereotype and patriarchy system attached in both countries.

Mohd. Faheem's work titled *India-ASEAN Physical Linkages* focuses on the opportunities and challenges of physical connectivity between India and ASEAN. He argues that there are numerous constraints in the process of regional connectivity which must be overcome to reach the true potential of India-ASEAN relationship.

A.N. Sarkar in his paper *A Perspective on India-ASEAN Economic Engagements* presents a perspective on India-ASEAN economic engagements and highlights various aspects related to services sector and the ASEAN Economic Community.

M. Absar Alam and Sarfaraaj Nasir in their paper *India-ASEAN Transport Connectivity* examine the various mechanisms, bottlenecks and way ahead for enhancing transport connectivity between India and the ASEAN countries.

Faisal Ahmed and Farhan Alam in their work titled *Geo-economics of India's Engagements with Cambodia, Laos, Myanmar and Vietnam (CLMV)* identify six enablers—defence and security cooperation, exclusive economic zones, global value chains, cyber security, small and medium enterprises, and services sector—which can further deepen India's engagements with the CLMV, amid changing geo-political architecture and politico-economic alignments in the Indo-Pacific region. Their paper deciphers the geo-economic of India-CLMV engagements and argues that with more policy space to the enablers, further mutual advantages in economic and cultural spheres can be leveraged.

We take this opportunity to place on record our deep appreciation and gratefulness to all the contributors to this volume. Their scholarly contributions would surely add to the existing body of literature and discourses on India-ASEAN co-operation.

Faisal Ahmed
Mohd. Faheem

1

India's Act East Policy through Blue Economy Co-operation

Dedi Dinarto

Abstract

This paper assesses the prospects and challenges of co-operation between India and Indonesia on the issue of 'blue economy'. I argue that India should invigorate its bilateral relationship with Indonesia through the blue economy co-operation if it is to strengthen its 'Act East Policy'. In doing so, this chapter illustrates the evolution and status quo of India-Indonesia relationship. Thereafter, it examines the extent of Indonesia's economic development dependency on oceans and seas. Despite its geographical assets, firm doctrine, and strong policy framework, Indonesia still faces non-traditional maritime security threat to be solved. In conclusion, this chapter proposes recommendation for India to consider the gap Indonesia possessed in the security field as a potential gateway for strategic engagement.

Introduction

"We have to strive to restore Indonesia as a maritime country. The oceans, the seas, the straits, and the bays are our future. We have been turning our backs on them for too long. Now is the time to restore all until '*Jalesveva Jayamahe, in our seas we are triumphant*'—President of Indonesia, Joko Widodo. [1]

"Friends! India has had a glorious maritime history. We are on the path of shaping an even better maritime future. The maritime sector not only creates and facilitates economic activities; it also connects countries and civilizations"— Prime Minister of India, Narendra Modi. [2]

Oceans and seas have always been the central of human deeds. It served as the most important lane for global trade, where 10 billion tons of goods comprising of chemicals, gas, oil, containers, and minor and main bulk commodities were brought by means of marine transport. [3] These goods represent 80 percent of the total global trade, signifying that oceans and seas are prominent as a medium for transferring goods. [4] In this sense, the global trade is highly inseparable from the safety and security of oceans and seas. Oceans and seas also provide diversified and nutritious food for human consumption. In 2014, fish utilization for food uses reached approximately 150 million tons, while non-food uses accounted for 20 million tons. [5]

In 2013, fish accounted for about 17 percent of animal protein consumed by global population, such as essential amino acids, fats, vitamins, and minerals. [6] Having said this, fisheries sector remains significant in contributing to global food security. Moreover, oceans and seas provide untapped resources of energy and minerals. In fact, human activities on oceans and seas, such as over-fishing, by catch, micro-plastics pollution, offshore oil and gas operations, and deep-sea mining, are inevitable to cause environmental damage towards oceans and seas.

Given the fact of global concern over harnessing the economic potential of oceans and at the same time preventing the environmental risk of marine fisheries and transportation, the concept of 'blue economy' has been widely adopted. As an innovative and new concept firstly introduced at the Rio+20 United Nations Conference on Sustainable Development in 2012, many countries considered this approach reliable to develop coastal and marine resources management. Promoted by the Small Island Developing States (SIDS), whose sovereignty and survival are highly dependable on seas, oceans, and climate change, these countries not only highlighted the importance to harness marine resources, but also emphasized the destructive impact of human activities over the coastal and marine ecosystem. The leading country to implement 'blue economy' is the Republic of Seychelles, an African country located on the Western Indian Ocean. Seychelles has been assisted by the Commonwealth Secretariat to authenticate the Blue Economy Strategic Roadmap, moving itself towards a more integrated ocean-based economy. [7]

'Blue economy' signifies a model of sustainable development, which combines the utilization of coastal and marine ecosystem along with the protection of marine environment. Besides, the concept of 'blue economy' has been widely defined. The Indian Ocean Rim Association (IORA) describes 'blue economy' as "a driver for sustainable development; research and development; investment; technology transfer; with focus on capacity building to increase the potential of ocean for socio-economic benefit". [8]

Christian Bueger examined some definition of 'blue economy', where many important keywords are found, such as business model, environment, social benefits, financial revenues, interdependent marine industries, sustainability, and centrality of the oceans for development. He concluded that 'blue economy' remains an interpretive concept with its distinctive characteristic of use, showing how the meaning of a concept is dependent on communities of users and their attempts to use them as tools in response to practical situations. [9] Practically, Jivanta Schottli emphasizes some potential marine sectors which are highly related to the implementation of 'blue economy', such as harvesting of living resources (fisheries), extraction and generation of non-living resources (deep seabed mining, oil and gas exploration), commerce and trade in and around the ocean (shipping, ports, tourism), as well as management of the ocean's health. [10] In general, 'blue economy' can be understood as an integrated marine-based approach for socio-economic development to achieve sustainability of ocean management and utilization.

Among many other countries, India started to eye the

importance of blue economy concept during India's Prime Minister Narendra Modi's visit to Seychelles, Mauritius, and Sri Lanka. He urged for co-operation in blue economy to exploit hydrocarbons and other marine resources; deep-sea fishing; preservation of marine ecology; and mitigating climate change by addressing environmental issues and disaster management. [11] Following this issue, Raja Mohan assessed that the way India expands co-operation on the blue economy is a way to broaden its sphere of influence in the Indian Ocean. [12] The focus on blue economy is also included as one of Modi's five-fold dimensions for Indian Ocean, among the others such as defending and securing India's maritime interests, strengthening security co-operation with regional partners, building multilateral co-operative maritime security in the Indian Ocean, and opening up of possibility to co-operate with great powers. Acknowledged by the Chief Executive of Nature Seychelles, Nirmal Jivan Shah, India is considered to have the most to offer to Seychelles in terms of the blue economy, such as lending expertise for deep seabed activities, hydrographic surveys, and weather predictions. [13]

Southeast Asia itself possesses a large potential for India to broaden its influence in the implementation of blue economy. Rajni Nayanthara Gamage argued that the implementation of blue economy would be the new potential for Southeast Asia's economic development. [14] He highlighted that Indonesia remains a regional champion as it has geographical assets, 'global maritime fulcrum' doctrine, and strong policy framework. Since Indonesia has been a historical partner in India's foreign policy, I argue that India should invigorate its bilateral relationship with Indonesia—a locus of India's interest in Southeast Asia—if it rethinks to expand its influence in Southeast Asia through the blue economy co-operation. Similarly, Srikanth Kondapalli perceived that Indonesia would be the factor of India's success in 'Act East Policy'. [15]

Against these backdrops, this chapter assesses the

prospects and challenges of co-operation between India and Indonesia on the issue of 'blue economy'. I argue that India should invigorate its bilateral relationship with Indonesia through the blue economy co-operation if it is to strengthen its 'Act East Policy'. In doing so, this chapter illustrates the evolution and status quo of India-Indonesia relationship. Thereafter, it examines the extent of Indonesia's economic development dependency on oceans and seas. Despite its geographical assets, firm doctrine, and strong policy framework, Indonesia still faces non-traditional maritime security threat to be solved. In conclusion, this chapter proposes recommendation for India to consider the gap Indonesia possesses in the security field as a potential gateway for strategic engagement.

Evolution and Status Quo of India-Indonesia Relationship

Indonesia has always been an important regional and global player for India's foreign policy. India and Indonesia are the two countries that have shared long historical trajectory, both in terms of economic and political aspects. From 1947 to 1966, India and Indonesia faced a dynamic relationship influenced by both national and international political factors. [16] Within the 'Period of Cordiality' from 1947 to 1958, India initiated to open a way to co-operation by fully supporting Indonesia to achieve its independence against colonialism. In 1951, both the countries signed a 'Treaty of Friendship' signifying high commitment to increase diplomatic, military, and trade co-operation. It also marks a pathway for the birth of 'Bandung Conference', a non-aligned movement during the Cold War.

In early 1950s, India and Indonesia started to look at Communist China as a potential actor to be aligned within the Bandung Conference with its adherence to *Panchsheel* (Five Principles of Peaceful Co-existence). However, this perspective was unlikely to be preserved by India realizing that the boundary dispute with China, the Tibetan uprising in 1959, and India's moral support to Tibet started the conflict between the two countries. In contrary, Indonesia remained firm that Communist China is an anti-imperialist power with whom it was worth co-operating. The situation kept worsening when Indonesia refused to grant visas to the team from Nationalist China for the Asian Games, to keep Communist China happy, and at the same time showing its anger towards India.

In 1965, the reconfiguration of domestic politics in Indonesia led to changes in foreign policy orientation. Having Sukarno's pro-Peking stance stimulated caution from the army, which eventually resulted in bloodstained killings of the Indonesian Communist Party (PKI) leaders by the army and the right-wing Muslim fanatics. Afterwards, Sukarno was forced to transfer his authority to Suharto. Under the command of President Suharto, Indonesia wiped out diplomatic relations with China and repaired the damaged diplomatic relations with India. Although this historical event led to the mass killing of the PKI's members, it served as a platform for deeper bilateral co-operation between India and Indonesia.

The first mutual understanding between the two countries started when they acknowledged UN Declaration on Indian Ocean as a 'peace zone' in 1971. On August 8, 1974, India and Indonesia signed co-operation agreement on sea demarcation within the Nicobar and Sumatran seas. Afterwards, the two countries added some sea demarcation lines on January 14, 1977, which was then followed by the signing of Tri-Junction Point on June 22, 1978 together with Thailand. One year later, the two countries agreed to establish special multi-disciplinary forces to study economic and industrial co-operation and collaboration. On December 1, 1980, President Suharto visited India and opined:

"To us, India is not merely a nation that has inherited a highly civilized history and culture and had established relations with Indonesia many centuries ago. To us, India is a friend, our close friend. As friends, as comrades-in-arms and as fellow members of the Non-Aligned Movement, the two countries must intensify co-operation for the advancement of our respective people and also for the betterment of the world". [17]

In 1990s, India's "Look East Policy" was unveiled to secure India's interest in Southeast Asia, where India engaged with some multilateral bodies like ASEAN and ASEAN Regional Forum (ARF). Considered as an economic powerhouse after its economic reforms in 1991, India had been known as a viable economic partner, particularly by Indonesia when the Asian financial crisis hit the country. Interestingly, India viewed Indonesia as a 'gateway' or 'lynchpin state' for India's regional interest in Southeast Asia. [18] This produces an asymmetrical relation between the two countries.

Since then, the strong established relationship between the two countries was a result of intensive diplomacy. In 2003, the India-Indonesia Joint Commission agreed to create a Plan of Action for enhancing strategic engagement. The two countries explored potential fields for co-operation, such as special economic zone development, alternative energy resources, health and pharmacy, gas and oil, mining, and biotechnology. This co-operation was boosted by the establishment of Joint Study Group (JSG) on Comprehensive Economic Cooperation Agreement (CECA) when Indonesian President Susilo Bambang Yudhoyono visited India in 2005.

In January 2011, President Yudhoyono intensified the bilateral co-operation by visiting India as the chief guest on India's Republic Day. During the visit, they agreed to set up an India-Indonesian Eminent Persons Group (II-EPG). It was aimed to review India-Indonesia relations and explore ways to widen and deepen the existing co-operation towards a sustainable long-term strategic partnership between India and Indonesia. Some fields taken into consideration included defence, home, oil and gas, coal, power, renewable energy, science and technology, tourism, health and education. In addition, the two sides also agreed to organize a Trade and Investment Forum, and a CEO's Forum.

The agreement was thus manifested in the era of President

Joko Widodo, whose foreign policy was to focus on economic diplomacy. A 25-member high-powered business delegation accompanied the President while he paid a visit to New Delhi from December 11-13, 2016. Boosting of economic engagement with special focus on pharmaceuticals and IT was the main business agenda of the visit. On the sidelines of the visit, the meeting of India-Indonesia CEOs' Forum was held in New Delhi on December 12, 2016. The forum discussed and arrived at constructive suggestions to enhance bilateral trade and investment co-operation. It was agreed by both the sides to set up sectoral core groups to suggest specific recommendations to institute strategies for expanding co-operation in identified sectors and to take up any impediments to trade and investment with both governments.

Additionally, a select group of twenty Indian CEOs met President Joko Widodo on December 13, 2016 during which the President invited the Indian companies to invest in Indonesia and assured them that the Indonesian government will address issues if any on a priority basis. Besides the focus engagement on trade and investment forum, the bilateral co-operation between India and Indonesia was directed to work on maritime issues. The two countries signed three MoUs, in which one of the three focused on illegal, unregulated and unreported (IUU) fishing to promote sustainable fisheries governance with the additional joint statement on maritime co-operation. In conclusion, it is safe to say that the strong diplomatic ties have been established between the two countries which included many issues ranging from economy, politics, and security, even though the bilateral relationship is more directed and dominated by India compared to Indonesia.

Is Indonesia's *Blue* Enough to Invigorate India's Act East Policy?

Indonesia is among the notable countries whose policy framework has experienced great turn since the reign of President Joko Widodo. Bringing along the 'global maritime fulcrum' vision, Indonesia puts an effort to reconsider its maritime domain, harnessing marine resources, strengthening maritime security, and intensifying maritime diplomacy. Thus, it is important to look at the extent of Indonesia's economic development dependency on oceans and seas to measure the potentiality of Indonesia as a 'lynchpin' state of India's broader interest in Southeast Asia.

As the world's largest archipelagic nation, with 5.8 million km^2 of territorial water and 17,508 islands, the oceans are a vital sector of Indonesia's statehood, forming an essential part of the country's economy, culture, and identity. Till date, Indonesia has been globally ranked at third place with a total coastline of 54,716 km. after Canada and Norway. [19] According to the report from Food and Agriculture Organization of the United Nations, Indonesia remained the second major producer of marine capture worth 6,016,525 tons in 2014. [20] In term of aquaculture, Indonesia produced 4,253,900 tons contributing to 5.77 percent of global total production in 2014. In 2004, the total export of fish and aquatic products resulted in significant foreign exchange earnings of US$ 1,643,542 for Indonesia. [21]

Moreover, Indonesia possesses abundant non-living resources as other strategic marine resources. Richardson noted that Indonesian coastal areas and oceans produce about 70 percent of oil and gas production. [22] He revealed that among the 60 basins holding potential of containing oil and gas, 40 basins are offshore basins, 14 basins are on the coast, and only 6 basins are on the mainland. Indonesia is also a home for new type of energy substitute in the form of gas hydrates and biogenic gases, specifically located off the west coast of Sumatra and at the southern West Java. In addition, the natural hydropower is also being utilized, under which Indonesia successfully produced hydropower capacity worth 5,258 MW in 2015. [23] Indonesian maritime sector is also contributing to the deeds of nation. The ocean economy of Indonesia comprised roughly 14.85 percent of the nation's

GDP in 2014. [24] In term of workforce, the maritime sector absorbed 4.12 percent of the total workforce which stood at 107.8 million people. The largest contribution comes from sub-sectors of roads, bridges, and ports amounting to 1.65 percent of the national economy.

Besides the great potential of its geographical assets and maritime sector development, Indonesia adopted 'global maritime fulcrum' (GMF) doctrine, a grand vision promoted by President Joko Widodo that has gained criticism among notable scholars. Despite its strong conceptualization and realization, the sustainability of this grand project is highly dependable on external supports in the form of funding and investments. [25] Another issue is that this strong doctrine lacks vibrant blueprint and master plan. [26] Although Indonesia's National Medium Term Development Plan (RPJMN) as the general guideline of national development has outlined the country's maritime aspirations, its focus on overall development policy makes it far too broad to serve as a guideline for the GMF stakeholders.

However, those issues have been resolved by the issuance of Presidential Regulation No. 16/2017, which strongly emphasizes the national commitment to revitalize its maritime domain. In a specific scope, the Ministry of Marine and Fisheries (*Kementerian Kelautan dan Perikanan*) adopted a strong doctrine to support the implementation of GMF, which emphasizes the nexus of sovereignty, sustainability, and prosperity. It was highlighted in the Ministry of Marine Affairs (MMAF) 2015-2019 Strategic Plan with detailed explanation, as follows:

1. 'Sovereignty' emphasizes firm opposition against the practice of illegal, unreported and unregulated (IUU) fishing, which shall be combated by sinking captured vessels. The specific task force is established to take the responsibility of preventing and combating IUU fishing.
2. 'Sustainability' highlights the protection of marine and fisheries resources through legal measures.
3. 'Prosperity' accentuates the utilization of marine and coastal resources to improve the well-being of

beneficiaries and stakeholders, such as exporters, fish farmers, fishermen, and processors.

This strong policy framework adopted by the Indonesian Ministry of Marine and Fisheries brought significant changes to the management of marine resources. Since the combat against IUU fishing was being implemented, the fisheries sector significantly grew by 8.37 percent on a year-on-year basis in the third quarter of 2015, outpacing the national economic growth with a 4.73 percent year-on-year growth. [27] According to a study by the National Commission on Fish Stock Research, the maximum sustainable yield (MSY) increased from 7.3 million tons in 2015 to 9.93 million tons in 2016. [28] The export value also experienced a similar trend with an increased value of 5.8 percent from US$ 3.94 million in 2015 to US$ 4.17 million in 2016. Despite the criticism towards the approach taken by the Minister of Marine and Fisheries Susi Pudjiastuti upon the welfare of traditional fishermen in Bitung that imposes the prohibition of transhipment, this prodigious achievement should be seen as a significant reform in the field of marine and fisheries sector.

Indonesia itself has also focussed on the implementation of blue economy. In 2012, the Indonesian President Susilo Bambang Yudhoyono declared to implement 'blue economy' concept in the Rio+20 meeting in Brazil. This concern departed from the awareness not only to develop marine and fisheries, but also to support the rapid development with zero carbon emissions, less environmental impact, and zero waste. By 2012, Indonesia poured approximately 38.8 billion IDR in the blue economy project implemented in Bali. Indonesia has also displayed its blue economy concept reflecting from its implementation in East Lombok and Central Lombok at the Food and Agriculture Organization of the United Nations, highlighting an integrated development program covering tuna fisheries, aquacultures, marine tourism, salt and pearl industries. [29]

The Lombok Blue Economy Implementation Programme

itself is expected to create 77,700 new jobs and generating income to the tune of US$ 114.88 million per year. [30] The firm commitment was shown seriously, when Indonesia hosted the second Indian Ocean Rim Association (IORA) Blue Economy Ministerial Conference. Indonesia urged IORA members not only to have exchange of views on blue economy, but also to jointly work in implementing the blue economy in five areas of co-operation, namely fisheries and aquaculture, inter-port co-operation, customs co-operation, maritime tourism, and marine plastic wastes. [31]

Not only displaying the strong commitment at national level to implement 'blue economy', Indonesia also recently took some initiatives to promote this new development approach in ASEAN. Coordinating Minister of Maritime Affairs Luhut Binsar Pandjaitan called all ASEAN member states to resolve ocean garbage, which has caused loss to the tune of US$ 1.2 billion to fisheries, shipping, tourism, and insurance business sectors. [32] Indonesia has taken a serious commitment to reduce 70 percent of its ocean waste by 2025, pledging US$ 1 billion a year. [33] In 2014, Indonesia also facilitated business deals on marine resources management and fishery products by organizing the World Ocean Business Forum (WOBF), which served as a platform for the stakeholders engaged in seaweed trading to prepare the ASEAN's Senior Official Meeting (SOM) on seaweed development cooperation. [34]

Having said these, Indonesia must be considered as a potential partner with whom India could broaden its blue economy implementation in Southeast Asia. The strong commitment given by Indonesia at both national and regional level provides a gateway for India to contribute and enlarge its political influence in the region. However, as outlined by Gamage, the ASEAN Way as a means and mechanism of regional decision-making indicates institutional constraints although Indonesia would be the initial partner of India for the blue economy co-operation. [35] In this sense, ASEAN comprehends the various interests and stakes of each individual state, in which Ebarvia perceived that ASEAN member countries have much work to be done if it has to form a single framework of blue economy implementation in Southeast Asia. [36] Not to underestimate the current progress, India could still consider Indonesia with its potential progress of blue economy in Southeast Asia, though India must fill the contemporary challenges faced by Indonesia.

Indonesia's Challenges on Blue Economy Implementation: Prospect for India's Contribution

Despite its potential to develop blue economy initiative, the Indonesian maritime domain serves as a growing spot of non-traditional threat against maritime security, particularly illegal, unreported, and unregulated (IUU) fishing, and piracy and armed robbery against ships. Although Gamage argued that non-traditional security threat might not impede the implementation of blue economy initiative, in the particular case of Indonesia, this chapter strongly argues that those non-traditional security threats will impede the maximization of blue economy implementation. Ranging from the loss of valuable goods, such as cargo, hauls, international commodities to the life of seafarers, these need to be highlighted as important factors for the implementation of blue economy initiative.

Indonesia is home to the two most emerging threats in the region, namely the IUU fishing, and piracy and armed robbery against ships. Since 2013, Indonesia has suffered losses of around US$ 3 billion a year from rampant illegal fishing activities. [37] The most prone areas where IUU often occurs is in the Arafura Sea, while not neglecting that it also happens in Java Sea and some sea borders in Borneo. [38] However, since Susi Pudjiastuti has headed the Ministry of Marine and Fisheries, she had shed light to fight against the IUU fishing practice. Indonesia's firm stance to combat IUU fishing has brought regional and global attention due to its hard treatment by exploding and sinking the IUU fishing vessels. The recent update reported that Indonesia has sunk 81 more vessels involved in illegal fishing. [39] Though this measure has been appreciated, Indonesia has also intensified its fight through technological co-operation with Australia. The usage of radar and satellites monitoring the IUU fishing helps the Indonesian Naval Army to crack down on illegal vessels. [40]

A memorandum of understanding between the Indonesian government and Spire Global, the satellite-powered data company, has also been signed to locate illegal fishing vessels. [41] The Indonesian government also lured the attention of United Nations by pointing out the importance of a designated body to ensure the "right of oceans" out of political agenda. [42] As mentioned previously, the result is a significant rise in Indonesia's yield and export of fisheries.

Despite the notable achievement from Indonesian government to combat the IUU fishing, the attention to fight piracy and armed robbery against ships remains low. At the global scale, piracy and armed robbery against ship remains high. Data shown in Table 1.1 illustrates the number of attacks by pirates as listed in the International Maritime Organization's (IMO) data collection system based on the area of attack.

Table 1.1: List of Piracy and Armed Robbery against Ships Based on Area of Incident, 2012-2016 [44]

Year	International Seas		Territorial Seas		Port Areas		Total of Piracy and Armed Robbery against Ships
2016	44	27 %	21	13 %	96	60 %	161
2015	36	12 %	141	46.5 %	126	41.5 %	303
2014	82	28 %	118	41 %	90	31 %	290
2013	70	23 %	51	17 %	182	60 %	303
2012	127	36 %	73	21 %	152	43 %	352

Two areas that are vulnerable to piracy are territorial sea and state ports. From 2012 to 2016, attacks also occurred in international sea areas with an average attack of 25 percent of the total attacks. Although IMO has promoted the use of the

International Ship and Port Facility Security Code (ISPS Code) in 2004 to improve port's loading and unloading security, this does not directly prevent piracy and reduce armed robbery against ships. According to a report released by the World Bank in 2013 entitled *Pirates of Somalia: Ending the Threat, Rebuilding a Nation*, it was noted that piracy activities and armed robbery against ships have cost the world trade an average of US$ 18 billion annually. [43]

In Southeast Asia, according to a report from Dryad, a private intelligence agency, piracy in the region has increased by 22 percent compared to 2014. [45] From 1995 to 2013, Southeast Asia accounted for 40 percent of the total piracy in world due to many strategic areas used opportunistically by the pirates, particularly in the shipping lanes of the Malacca Strait, the Singapore Strait and South China Sea. [46] From the number of cases, Indonesia ranks first in Southeast Asia. According to the report of ICC International Maritime Bureau (Table 1.2), Indonesia occupies the highest position in the area where the piracy activity occurs. From 2011 to 2015, there has been a significant increase of 134 percent in Indonesia. Compared to other parts of Southeast Asia, Indonesia with its overlapped jurisdiction with three major trade routes in Southeast Asia, remained vulnerable to the pirate attacks. Let alone, the port is a preferred place for most of the piracy and armed robbery against ships in Indonesia (Table 1.3). The percentage of incidents of piracy and armed robbery against ships in ports sequentially reached 65 percent of the total cases in 2012, 79 percent in 2013, 77 percent in 2014, and 82 percent in 2015. This data highlights that ports in Indonesia are vulnerable areas targeted by the pirates.

Concerned with the situation of potential threat from piracy and armed robbery against ships in Indonesia following the implementation of blue economy initiative, the Indonesian government has to draw its attention towards the provision of resources to enhance the maritime security. Resources covering capabilities for both marine and air fleet systems, as well as personnel with adequate experience and training, are essentially needed. The Marine Security Agency (Badan Keamanan Laut/Bakamla) as a civil institution enforcing the law of the sea in Indonesia is practically limited in terms of resources.

Table 1.2: Piracy in Indonesia Based on Places, 2011-2015 [47]

Location		2011	2012	2013	2014	2015
Southeast Asia	Indonesia	46	81	106	100	108
	Malaysia	16	12	9	24	13
	Myanmar	1	-	-	-	-
	Philippines	5	3	3	6	11
	Malacca Strait	11	6	9	8	9
	Thailand	-	-	-	2	1

Table 1.3: Number of Attacks against Ships in Indonesian Ports, 2012-2015 [48][49][50][51]

Ports	2012 (81 cases)	2013 (106 cases)	2014 (100 cases)	2015 (108 cases)
Adang Bay	4	4	-	-
Balikpapan	3	5	-	-
Batam	3	-	-	-
Belawan	14	18	9	15
Dumai	11	12	-	5
Gresik	-	4	-	-
Jakarta/Tanjung Priok	7	6	9	4
Karimun Besar/Kecil	-	-	18	24
Muara Berau	4	4	6	-
Muara Jawa	-	4	-	-
Nipah	-	14	-	26
Pulau Bintan	-	-	35	
Pulau Takong Kecil	-	-	-	11
Samarinda	-	5	-	-
Taboneo	7	8	-	4
Total	53 cases	84 cases	77 cases	89 cases
Percentage	65 %	79 %	77 %	82 %

Since the beginning, Bakamla received financial support from the central government with a total budget of 520 billion Indonesian rupiah a year plus three patrol boats, which was then enhanced with the approval of the House of

Representatives to 726.3 billion Indonesian rupiah annually with the addition of another 30 patrol boats. [52] With vast stretch of waters, it is still not safe to say that the current resources are enough to ensure the security of Indonesia's maritime domain against piracy and armed robbery. Bakamla also lacks human resources. According to Bakamla's Head of Operations Management Colonel Andi Achdar, the most sought after resources not owned by Bakamla are human resources, which result in weak formulation of national policies in the field of security and safety, the organization of early warning systems, maintenance and supervision, and monitoring. [53] With these limitations, it is impossible for Bakamla to perform all the functions within a wide range of working areas.

In this sense, the downsides of Indonesia's maritime security to fight piracy and armed robbery against ships would serve as a potential platform for India to involve in strategic co-operation with Indonesia. The achievement of the Ministry of Marine and Fisheries to combat illegal, unreported, and unregulated (IUU) fishing should not be over-appreciated, let alone the issue of piracy and armed robbery against ships in Indonesia which is still unresolved and sets aside a national agenda for resolution.

Although India-Indonesia Coordinated Patrol (CORPAT) has become a continuous solution regards the maritime security problem in the Indian Ocean, which have been held since 2002, yet, this bilateral exercise between the two countries' should be reframed to include the blue economy initiative as a standard procedure for both the navies. As this exercise of co-operation has considered some blue economy related issues, such as combating unlawful activities, controlling pollution, and keeping safe and secure passage for commercial shipping, this exercise has the potential to be upgraded into a more strategic co-operation including intensive maritime patrol. Let alone, this platform could also boost monitoring and surveillance technology exchange.

In general, the result of Widodo's visit to New Delhi on December 12, 2016 must be considered as an important milestone where the two countries realized the importance of their shared geographical and maritime border along with all the potential threats, including illegal fishing. The two countries have also signed a Joint Statement on Maritime Cooperation, in which India and Indonesia clearly called for greater involvement and strategic co-operation within the sphere of maritime security co-operation. Therefore, India must not overlook the gap Indonesia possesses, as a potential platform for its strategic engagement with it—a gateway to its larger interest in Southeast Asia.

Conclusion

In conclusion, this chapter has examined the prospects and challenges of co-operation between India and Indonesia on the issue of 'blue economy'. Indonesia as a notable country in Southeast Asia with strong willingness to implement and promote the blue economy initiative holds potential for India to broaden its influence in the blue economy implementation. India should invigorate its bilateral relationship with Indonesia through the blue economy co-operation if it is to strengthen its 'Act East Policy'. It is also safe to say that strong diplomatic ties have been established between the two countries which included many issues ranging from economy, politics, and security, even though the bilateral relationship is more directed and dominated by India compared to Indonesia—the result of India's perception towards Indonesia as a lynchpin state.

Moreover, Indonesia's economic development highly depends on oceans and seas, making it a potential entity to implement the blue economy initiative. As the world's largest archipelagic nation, with 5.8 million km^2 of territorial water and 17,508 islands, the oceans are a vital sector of Indonesia's statehood, forming an essential part of the country's economy, culture, and identity. Both Global Maritime Fulcrum's doctrine and MMAF 2015-2019 Strategic Plan have served as two notable policy frameworks for the blue economy implementation. Indonesia must be considered as a potential partner where India could broaden its blue economy implementation in Southeast Asia. The strong commitment given by Indonesia at both national and regional level provides a gateway for India to contribute and enlarge its political influence in the region.

Not to underestimate the current progress of blue economy initiative made by Indonesia, India must fill the contemporary challenges faced by Indonesia. Since Indonesian maritime domain serves as a growing spot of non-traditional threat against maritime security, particularly illegal, unreported, and unregulated (IUU) fishing, and piracy and armed robbery against ships, India must fill this position as to make it a relevant partner for Indonesia to encounter non-traditional maritime security threat.

Endnotes

1. "Jokowi's Inaugural Speech as Nation's Seventh President", *Jakarta Globe*, available at: http://jakartaglobe.id/news/jokowis-inaugural-speech-nations-seventh-president.
2. Modi, N., "India Has Had a Glorious Maritime History; We Are On the Path of Shaping an Even Better Maritime Future: PM", *Narendra Modi* (online), 14 April 2016, available at: http://www.narendramodi.in/pm-modi-at-the-inauguration-of-maritime-india-summit-2016-in-mumbai-440341.
3. United Nations Conference on Trade and Development, "Review of Maritime Transport", United Nations Publication, New York, 2016, p. 6.
4. United Nations Conference on Trade and Development, "Review of Maritime Transport", United Nations Publication, New York, 2016, p. 7.
5. Food and Agriculture Organization of the United Nations, "The State of World Fisheries and Aquaculture: Contributing to Food Security and Nutrition for All", FAO, Rome, 2016, p. 3.
6. Food and Agriculture Organization of the United Nations, "The State of World Fisheries and Aquaculture: Contributing to Food Security and Nutrition for All", FAO, Rome, 2016, p. 4.
7. "Seychelles Blue Economy Strategic Roadmap and

Implementation,' *The Commonwealth* (online), available at: http://thecommonwealth.org/project/seychelles-blue-economy-strategic-roadmap-and-implementation.

8. "Blue Economy: Introduction", *Indian Ocean Rim Association* (online), available at: http://www.iora.net/blue-economy/blue-economy.aspx.
9. Bueger, C. (2017), "Concepts in Practice: The Case of the 'Blue Economy", in P. Ish-Shalom (ed.), 'Concepts in Action/at Work: On the Meaning of Concepts in International Politics'.
10. Schottli, J. (2016), "India's Maritime Turn: A Blue Economy Strategy in the Making?", *ISAS Insights*, No. 332, p. 2.
11. Sharma, A.B. (2015), "Modi's New Ocean Politics: Gluing Security and the Blue Economy", *The Jakarta Post* (online), available at: http://www.thejakartapost.com/news/2015/03/31/modi-s-new-ocean-politics-gluing-security-and-blue-economy.html.
12. Mohan, C.R. (2015), "Modi and the Indian Ocean: Restoring India's Sphere of Influence", *Asia Maritime Transparency Initiative* (online), available at: https://amti.csis.org/modi-and-the-indian-ocean-restoring-indias-sphere-of-influence.
13. "Blue Economy and the Environment: If We Want the Game to Change then India is a Game Changer", *Nature Seychelles* (online), available at: http://natureseychelles.org/knowledge-centre/news-and-stories/latest-news/659-blue-economy-and-the-environment-if-we-want-the-game-to-change-then-india-is-a-game-changer.
14. Gamage, R.N. (2016), "Blue Economy in Southeast Asia: Oceans as the New Frontier of Economic Development", *Maritime Affairs: Journal of the National Maritime Foundation of India*, available at: http://dx.doi.org/10.1080/09733159.2016.1244361.
15. Ganapathy, N. (2016), "Maritime Security Drives Push for Closer India-Indonesia Ties", *Straits Times* (online), available at: http://www.straitstimes.com/asia/maritime-security-drives-push-for-closer-india-indonesia-ties.
16. Singh, L.P. (1967), "Dynamics of Indian-Indonesian Relations", *Asian Survey*, Vol. 7, No. 9, pp. 655-666.
17. Bhattacharya, S.S. (1981), "India-Indonesia Relations",

Strategic Analysis, Vol. 4, No. 11, p. 521.

18. Shekhar, V. (2010), "India and Indonesia: Reliable Partners in an Uncertain Asia", *Asia-Pacific Review*, Vol. 17, No. 2, pp. 76-98.
19. "Coastline Length" (2017), *World by Map* (online), available at: http://world.bymap.org/Coastlines.html.
20. Food and Agriculture Organization of the United Nations (2016), "The State of World Fisheries and Aquaculture: Contributing to Food Security and Nutrition for All", FAO, Rome, p. 11.
21. International Business Publication (2015), "Indonesia Fishing and Aquaculture Industry Handbook: Strategic Information, Regulations, Opportunities", IBP: Washington DC, p. 90.
22. Richardson, A.J. (2008), "In Hot Water: Zooplankton and Climate Change", *ICES Journal of Marine Science*, Vol. 65, pp. 279-295.
23. World Energy Council (2016), "World Energy Resources", WEC, New York, p. 42.
24. Suparmoko, M. (2016), "The Role of the Ocean Economy in the National Income Accounts of Indonesia", *Journal of Ocean and Coastal Economics*, Vol. 2, No. 2, p. 2.
25. RSIS (2015), "Indonesia's Global Maritime Fulcrum Challenges and Trajectories", *RSIS Event Report*, Singapore.
26. Marzuki, K. and Priamarizki, A. (2016), "Indonesia's Maritime Ambitions Remain Rudderless", *East Asia Forum* (online), available at: http://www.eastasiaforum.org/2016/09/02/indonesias-maritime-ambitions-remain-rudderless.
27. "Growth of Indonesia's Fishery Sector Outpacing Overall Economic Growth" (2015), *Indonesia-Investments* (online), available at: https://www.indonesia-investments.com/news/todays-headlines/growth-of-indonesia-s-fishery-sector-outpacing-overall-economic-growth/item6324?
28. "Naik 26,3 Persen, Stok Ikan Lestari Capai 12,5 Juta Ton", (2017), *Tempo Bisnis* (online), available at: https://bisnis.tempo.co/read/news/2017/06/01/090880514/naik-26-3-persen-stok-ikan-lestari-capai-12-5-juta-ton?source=graboards.com.
29. Lingga, V. (2014), "Indonesia Showcases Its Blue Economy

Projects in Fisheries at FAO", *The Jakarta Post* (online), available at:
http://www.thejakartapost.com/news/2014/06/10/indonesia-showcases-its-blue-economy-projects-fisheries-fao.html.

30. Soesilo, I. (2014), "Blue Economy for Marine Resource Development", *The Jakarta Post* (online), available at: http://www.thejakartapost.com/news/2014/03/20/blue-economy-marine-resource-development.html.
31. Dwinanda, R. (2017), "Indonesia Holds Second IORA Blue Economy Ministerial Conference", *Republika* (online), available at:
http://en.republika.co.id/berita/en/national-politics/17/05/08/opn1mo414-indonesia-holds-second-iora-blue-economy-ministerial-conference.
32. "ASEAN Must Cooperate More to Combat Plastic Waste: Minister" (2017), *The Jakarta Post* (online), available at: http://www.thejakartapost.com/news/2017/06/06/asean-must-cooperate-more-to-combat-plastic-waste-minister.html.
33. Langenheim, J. (2017), "Indonesia Pledges US$ 1 bn a Year to Curb Ocean Waste", *The Guardian* (online), available at: https://www.theguardian.com/environment/the-coral-triangle/2017/mar/02/indonesia-pledges-us1-billion-a-year-to-curb-ocean-waste.
34. "Government Promotes Blue Economy Based Investment" (2014), *Antara News* (online), available at: http://www.antaranews.com/en/news/94041/government-promotes-blue-economy-based-investment.
35. Gamage, R.N. (2016), "Blue Economy in Southeast Asia: Oceans as the New Frontier of Economic Development", *Maritime Affairs: Journal of the National Maritime Foundation of India*, available at:
http://dx.doi.org/10.1080/09733159.2016.1244361.
36. Ebarvia, M.C.M. (2016), "Economic Assessment of Oceans for Sustainable Blue Economy Development", *Journal of Ocean and Coastal Economics*, Vol. 2, No. 2.
37. Rosalina (2013), "Indonesia Suffers Rp 30 Trillion Loss from Illegal Fishing", *Tempo* (online), available at: https://en.tempo.co/read/news/2013/05/14/056480409/Indonesia-Suffers-Rp-30-Trillion-Loss-from-Illegal-Fishing.
38. Resosudarmo, B.P., Napitupulu, L. and Campbell, D. (2009),

"Illegal Fishing in the Arafura Sea", in B.P. Resosudarmo and F. Jotza (eds.), 'Working with Nature against Poverty: Development, Resources and the Environment in Eastern Indonesia', Institute of Southeast Asian Studies, Singapore.

39. "81 More Vessels Sunk over Illegal Fishing", (2017), *The Jakarta Post* (online), available at: http://www.thejakartapost.com/news/2017/04/01/81-more-vessels-sunk-over-illegal-fishing.html.
40. Smith, B. (2017), "Joint Action by Australia and Indonesia to Curb Illegal Fishing Hailed", *Sydney Morning Herald*, available at: http://www.smh.com.au/technology/sci-tech/joint-action-by-australia-and-indonesia-to-curb-illegal-fishing-hailed-20150819-gj3axx.html.
41. "Indonesia to Use Satellite Data to Pinpoint Locations of Illegal Fishing Vessels in Its Waters", (2016), *Straits Times*, available at: http://www.straitstimes.com/asia/se-asia/indonesia-to-use-satellite-data-to-pinpoint-locations-of-illegal-fishing-vessels-in-its.
42. Sulistiyono, A.G. (2017), "Indonesia Joins Global Effort to Curb Illegal Fishing", *The Jakarta Post* (online), available at: http://www.thejakartapost.com/news/2017/06/09/indonesia-joins-global-effort-to-curb-illegal-fishing.html.
43. Kermeliotis, T. (2013), "Somali Pirates Cost Global Economy '$18 Billion A Year", *CNN* (online), available at: http://edition.cnn.com/2013/04/12/business/piracy-economy-world-bank.
44. IMO (2016), "IMO Report 2012-2016 on Piracy and Armed Robbery against Ships", available at: https://gisis.imo.org/Public/PAR.
45. Graham, L. (2015), "Piracy Increases by 22% in Southeast Asia", *CNBC* (online), available at: http://www.cnbc.com/2015/07/09/piracy-increases-by-22-in-southeast-asia.html.
46. McCauley, A. (2014), "Southeast Asia: The Most Dangerous Waters in the World", *TIME* (online), available at: http://time.com/piracy-southeast-asia-malacca-strait.
47. ICC-IMB (2015), "Piracy and Armed Robbery against Ships Annual Report 2015", available at:

https://www.icc-ccs.org/piracy-reporting-centre/request-piracy-report.
48. ICC-IMB (2012), "Piracy and Armed Robbery against Ships", ICC-IMB, London.
49. ICC-IMB (2013), "Piracy and Armed Robbery against Ships", ICC-IMB, London.
50. ICC-IMB (2014), "Piracy and Armed Robbery against Ships", ICC-IMB, London.
51. ICC-IMB (2015), "Piracy and Armed Robbery against Ships", ICC-IMB, London.
52. Parameswaran, P. (2015), "Indonesia's Maritime Ambition: Can Jokowi Realise It?", *RSIS Commentary* (online), available at: https://www.rsis.edu.sg/wp-content/uploads/2015/03/CO15044.pdf.
53. Afrida, N. (2015), "Bakamla Trapped in Overlapping Agencies", *The Jakarta Post* (online), available at: <http://www.thejakartapost.com/news/2015/02/03/bakamla-trapped-overlapping-agencies.html.

2

Women's Rights in India and Indonesia

Maya Dania

Abstract

The issue of human rights for women can't be separated from the discourse of violation against woman (VAW). Within the ASEAN region, domestic violence against women is one of the most common but under-reported forms of violence. The majority of victims are women abused by their own husbands or intimate partners. In Indonesia, many forms of VAW are mostly related with sexual and physical tortures. India also shares a similar situation. Sexual violence, mostly formed in gang-rape, has worsened over the past several years. The two countries shared comparable circumstances: most VAW cases go unreported, largely because of cultural stigmas surrounding such incidents that could bring shame to victims and their families. This paper aims to compare women's rights situation between India and Indonesia by applying a qualitative method that collects, compares, and analyzes literature. Data is taken from official reports published by the governments and CSOs.

The paper shows that between the two countries, there are found: (i) inadequate legal frameworks addressing VAW, (ii) pervasive impunity for violence against women in the region due to lack of gender-sensitivity and gender-responsiveness in law enforcement, and the formal, semi-formal, parallel justice and alternative dispute resolution systems, (iii) large number of unreported cases of VAW due to limited awareness of existing laws, poor law enforcement, lack of support services to survivors such as health care, legal aid, and psychosocial counselling, and (iv) poor implementation of existing laws due to limited understanding and capacity of law enforcers, judiciary, local government, health care sector and others involved. Finally, the paper concludes that religion and domestic laws play a pivotal role to discriminate against women, making them more vulnerable to any violence and reducing their opportunities and access to any resources and services, which often results in a lower quality of life.

Introduction

The issue of human rights for women can't be separated from the discourse of violation against woman or VAW. VAW is acknowledged as a violation of human rights, transcends the boundaries of nationality, culture, religion, and even socio-economic status. VAW is also recognized as a form of inequality and priority issue for women around the world. According to the World Health Organization, in 1997, at least one in five women suffered rape or attempted rape in their lifetime. From 20 percent to 50 percent of the women interviewed in 24 countries reported physical violence from their male partners. Somehow, VAW, present in most societies, is still considered as a "common" thing and it has gone mostly unrecognized and even unreported at all. [1]

In Southeast Asian countries, women's rights are still becoming a major issue. Even though the term of human rights must be applied equally to all human beings, in reality, women's rights are generally less respected than those of men in terms of customs and traditions. Religion and domestic laws can also discriminate against women, making them more vulnerable to any violence and reducing their opportunities and access to any resources and services, which often results in a lower quality of life. A report from the United Nations for Women in Bangkok stated that violence against women in Southeast Asia is widespread in various forms and also across the ASEAN member countries.

It occurs at all levels—in the family, the community, the society, cross-regionally and trans-nationally. It takes physical, psychological and economic forms, from domestic violence, trafficking, rape and sexual assault, to sexual harassment, forced/child marriage, bride kidnapping, bride price, son preference, sex-selective abortions and other forms. [2] Violence against women and girls is a major health and human rights issue. At least one in five of the world's female population has been physically or sexually abused by a man or men at some point of time in their life. [3]

Started in early 20th century, particularly in 1993, the World Conference on Human Rights in Vienna, the 1994 World Conference on Population in and Development, and the 1995 Fourth World Conference on Women in Beijing, scholars and activists, especially those working in so-called developing nations, have come increasingly to view violence against women as a human rights issue rather than merely a criminal justice or a public health issue. This movement has somehow influenced the way Southeast Asian people perceive violence against women. In addition to recognizing the debilitating effects of physical and sexual violence perpetrated against women by the private actors, such as by partners or family members in their homes, or by acquaintances and strangers in the community, this paradigm focuses attention on violence perpetrated against women by soldiers during times of war and internal conflicts; sexual assaults perpetrated against women in state custody by law enforcement personnel; rapes perpetrated against women in refugee camps by other refugees, local police, and/or military personnel; the trafficking of women for sexual exploitation or for menial labour; and harmful traditional practices, such as forced marriages, genital cutting, honour crimes, suttee. [4]

Women issues have somehow also become the priority in ASEAN agenda as women status has somewhat challenged the future of ASEAN. Thus, this paper aims to explore women issue in ASEAN countries by particularly examining the women rights issue in Indonesia as the highlighted case. This paper also tries to connect ASEAN as one regional organization with other international organizations regarding women's rights issues. In Indonesia alone, the case of VAW has been increasing since 2010 and according to the Indonesian National Women Committee (*Komnas Perempuan)*, from 33 provinces in Indonesia, reported cases of VAW reached almost 1,20,000 compared to 2010 when as many as 1,06,000 cases were reported. The most significant cases were found in Central Java at 26,000, followed by East Java with almost 25,000 cases. In West Java and Jakarta, many cases of sexual violence were reported against women. [5]

VAW in the form of sexual violence against women in Indonesia is not limited to the recent era. It was noted that since the Japanese occupation era, many "organized" massive rapes towards Indonesian women occurred. Many victims not even gained any attention from people and other nations. Thus, ASEAN, with its commitment to women issues, should make a special agenda towards VAW and especially in relation to sexual violence.

ASEAN and Women's Rights

The Convention on the Elimination of all Forms of Discrimination against Women (CEDAW) is an international treaty adopted in 1979 by the United Nations General Assembly. Described as an international bill of rights for women, it came into force on September 3, 1981. Over fifty countries that have ratified the Convention have done so, subject to certain declarations, reservations, and objections. The Convention defines discrimination against women in the following terms: any distinction, exclusion or restriction made on the basis of sex which has the effect or purpose of impairing or nullifying the recognition, enjoyment or exercise by women, irrespective of their marital status, on a basis of equality of men and women, of human rights and fundamental freedoms in the political, economic, social, cultural, civil or any other field. [6]

The Convention on the Elimination of All Forms of

Discrimination against Women (CEDAW) also establishes an agenda of action for putting an end to sex-based discrimination, meaning that states must take measures to seek to eliminate prejudices and customs based on the idea of the inferiority or the superiority of one sex or on stereotyped role. States should ratify the Convention to enshrine gender equality into their domestic legislations, repeal all discriminatory provisions in their laws, and enact new provisions to guard discrimination against women. [7]

The Convention on the Elimination of All Forms of Discrimination against Women (CEDAW) views gender-based violence as a serious obstacle to human rights and fundamental freedoms by women. In its General Recommendation 19, CEDAW defines gender-based violence as "violence directed against a woman because she is a woman or which affects a woman disproportionately. It includes physical, mental or sexual harm or suffering, threats of such acts, coercion and other deprivations of liberty". The United Nations Declaration on Elimination of Violence against Women (DEVAW) uses the same definition of violence against women (VAW) as CEDAW, but adds that VAW includes gender-based violence "occurring both in public or private life". This means that violence in the family, in the community and violence perpetrated or condoned by the state, is considered VAW regardless of whether it occurs in private or public. [8]

According to the United Nations, violence against women can be described as follows:

1. Violence in the family includes domestic violence, battering, marital rape, incest, forced prostitution by the family, violence against domestic workers and girl children, sex-selective abortion and infanticide, female circumcision, bride price-related violence and religious-customary laws that are harmful to women and girls.
2. Violence in the community includes rape/sexual assault, sexual harassment, violence within institutions, trafficking and forced prostitution, violence against women migrant

workers, and pornography.

3. Violence perpetrated or condoned by the state includes violence against women in conflict, custodial violence, violence against refugees and internally displaced persons, and violence against women against indigenous and minority groups.

ASEAN member states are strongly committed to protect and promote the human rights of women. This commitment is manifested in the ratification of CEDAW by all ten member states. It has also sparked one important note that with the establishment of ASEAN Intergovernmental Commission on Human Rights (AICHR) and the ASEAN Human Rights Declaration, the Commission has openly and officially outlined women's protection and rights under the ASEAN framework by emphasizing the importance of ASEAN's efforts in promoting human rights, including the reaffirming of the Declaration of the Advancement of Women in the ASEAN Region that was previously stated in Bangkok on July 5, 1988 and the Declaration on the Elimination of Violence against Women in the ASEAN Region that was previously stated in Jakarta on June 30, 2004.

The 2004 Declaration on the Elimination of Violence against Women in the ASEAN Region recognizes that "violence against women both violates and impairs their human rights and fundamental freedom". It calls on member states to take "necessary measures to eliminate all forms of discrimination against women" and "intensify efforts to develop and improve existing legislative, educational and social measures and support services aimed at the prevention of violence against women". By these Declarations, strengthened by the establishment of AICHR in 2009 and ASEAN Declaration of Human Rights in 2012, ASEAN member states are obliged, and strongly committed to protect and promote human rights of women and have emphasized that Southeast Asian women should be well-protected in education, work, and health. Southeast Asian women are exceptionally defenceless by religion, culture, and tradition whenever they are experiencing themselves in the gender-based situations reflected in sectors mentioned before. [9]

Women's Rights in India

Indian women have been actually granted more rights to live in the country compared to men. There are several privilege laws to protect Indian women and entitle gender equality. The principle of gender equality is enshrined in the Indian Constitution in its Preamble, Fundamental Rights, Fundamental Duties and Directive Principles.

The Indian government has also made sure that the laws can be fully implemented in order to enhance development policies, plans, and programs for women advancement, mostly based on the ratification of the Convention on Elimination of All Forms of Discrimination against Women (CEDAW) in 1993.

Up to the present day, India has achieved several special initiatives for women. In January 1992, the government set up the National Commission for Women to study and monitor all matters relating to the Constitutional and legal safeguards provided for women, review the existing legislations to suggest amendments wherever necessary, and so on. Also, in 1992, the government passed the Reservation for Women in Local Self-Government to ensure one-third of the total seats for women in all elected offices in local bodies whether in rural areas or urban areas.

Further, the National Plan of Action for the Girl Child (1991-2000) was implemented to ensure survival, protection and development of the girl child with the ultimate objective of building up a better future for the girl child. Finally, in 2001, the Department of Women and Child Development in the Ministry of Human Resource Development prepared a "National Policy for the Empowerment of Women". The goal of this policy was to bring about the advancement, development and empowerment of women. [10]

The Constitution of India grants Fundamental Rights to ensure equality before law and equal protection of law for Indian women. In brief, Articles 14, 15, 15(3), 16, 39(a), 39(b), 39(c), and 42 of the Constitution state the privileges for Indian women: [11]

1. Equality before law for women (Article 14).
2. The State is not to discriminate against any citizen on grounds of religion, race, caste, sex, place of birth or any of them [Article 15(i)].
3. The State to make any special provision in favour of women and children [Article 15(3)].
4. Equality of opportunity for all citizens in matters relating to employment or appointment to any office under the State (Article 16).
5. The State to direct its policy towards securing for men and women equally the right to an adequate means of livelihood [Article 39(a)]; and equal pay for equal work for both men and women [Article 39(d)].
6. To promote justice, on the basis of equal opportunity and to provide free legal aid by suitable legislations or schemes or in any other way to ensure that opportunities for securing justice are not denied to any citizen by reason of economic or other disabilities (Article 39A).
7. The State to make provision for securing just and humane conditions of work and for maternity relief (Article 42).
8. The Indian government has also enacted legal provisions to counter crime against women such as:

- Rape (Section 376 IPC).
- Kidnapping and abduction for different purposes (Sections 363-373).
- Homicide for dowry, dowry deaths or their attempts (Sections 302/304-B IPC).
- Torture—both mental and physical (Section 498-A IPC).
- Molestation (Section 354 IPC).
- Sexual harassment (Section 509 IPC).

To explain, in Indian Penal Code (IPC), a rapist, a person

who abducts, kills and causes bodily injury, uses criminal forces and cruelty, and also intends to insult a woman, shall be punished with rigorous imprisonment for years and may be extended to imprisonment for life, and shall also be liable to fine. The Indian government has also granted special laws for women some of which are as under:

- Dowry Prohibition Act, 1961, prohibits the request, payment, or acceptance of a dowry as consideration for marriage.
- Immoral Traffic Act, 1956, deals with the status of sex workers in private space and not in public space.
- Protection of Women from Domestic Violence Act, 2005, to protect women from domestic violence.
- Sexual Harassment of Women at Workplace (Prevention, Prohibition and Redressal) Act, 2013, to protect women from sexual harassment at their place of work.
- Family Courts Act, 1954, to conclude upon matters relating to family law like matrimonial reliefs, custody of children, maintenance for wife and children etc.
- Special Marriage Act, 1954, to provide a special form of marriage for the people of India and all Indian nationals in foreign countries with 3 major objectives: to provide a special form of marriage in certain cases, to provide for registration of certain marriages and to provide for divorce.
- Marriage Laws (Amendment) Bill, 2010, to amend the Hindu Marriage Act, 1955 and the Special Marriage Act, 1954, for making divorce easier on ground of irretrievable breakdown of marriage.
- Maternity Benefit Act, 1961, (amended in 1995) to entitle women maternity benefit.
- Medical Termination of Pregnancy (MTP) Act to reduce the incidence of illegal abortion and consequent maternal mortality and morbidity.
- Equal Remuneration Act, 1976, to provide for the payment of equal remuneration to men and women workers and for

the prevention of discrimination, on the ground of sex, against women in the matter of employment and for matters, connected there with or incidental thereto. [12]

Violence against Women in ASEAN Member States: A Case Study of Indonesia

Everyday women around the world are maligned, humiliated, assaulted, beaten, raped, physically tortured, threatened with weapons and murdered. In Indonesia, women share the same fate. Indonesian newspapers and television also often report about many cases of VAW like being battered, raped, assaulted, and even murdered.

However, although many reports stated that many women were being assaulted, attacked, raped, and even murdered in almost daily news in Indonesian media, it is difficult to estimate accurate figures of incidence of VAW suffered by the Indonesian women. There are some reasons of why an accurate number of reported cases are so hard to get.

Firstly, many Indonesian women, due to their culture, are often reluctant to report the actual incidents because they are terrified of being assaulted by their own families.

Indonesian women, especially the Javanese, adhere to the value that any family matter that brings shame should not be discussed in the public. Secondly, many women may have different opinions as to what type of behaviours can be categorized as violence.

Lastly, even if the women do report, the police often fails to record the incident of VAW unless it can be categorized as a crime. Therefore, even though VAW does exist, it is often underreported. [13] It is, thus, very important to understand the definition of VAW and make an accurate categorization of what perspective should be applied to examine various forms of VAW.

VAW can happen to women of any class, culture and of any age. Dimensions of VAW can be better understood from Table 2.1: [14]

Table 2.1: Violence against Women throughout the Life Cycle

Phase	Type of Violence
Pre-birth	Sex-selective abortion; effects of battering during pregnancy on birth outcomes
Infancy	Female infanticide; physical, sexual and psychological abuse
Girlhood	Child marriage; female genital mutilation; physical, sexual and psychological abuse; incest; child prostitution and pornography
Adolescence and dating and courtship violence	(e.g. acid throwing and date rape); adulthood economically coerced sex (e.g. school girls having sex with "sugar daddies" in return for school fees); incest; sexual abuse in the workplace; rape; sexual harassment; forced prostitution and pornography; trafficking in women; partner violence; marital rape; dowry abuse and murders; partner homicide; psychological abuse; abuse of women with disabilities; forced pregnancy
Elderly	Forced "suicide" or homicide of widows for economic reasons; sexual, physical and psychological abuse

Within the ASEAN region, domestic violence is one of the most common but underreported forms of violence. The overwhelming majority of victims in domestic violence cases are women abused by their husbands or intimate partners. Up to 95 percent of all cases of domestic violence in Vietnam and up to 96 percent in Indonesia are perpetrated by husbands against their wives. In Thailand, 44 percent of women reported that they have suffered sexual and/or physical abuse while in their current or former relationship. [15] Studies reveal that indigenous and ethnic minority women are disempowered by harmful practices combined with discriminatory attitudes and practices in mainstream society. [16]

In Indonesia, many forms of VAW are mostly related with

sexual violence against women. Presently, sexual violence against women in the form of rapes occurred in West Java and Jakarta. From the accumulated number of VAW reported officially, from as many as almost 300,000 cases in 2013, one-third or as many as 100,000 cases were marked by sexual violence and almost 80 percent of the cases suffered by Indonesian women were committed by their own close relatives, their fathers, their boyfriends, their husbands, or many other actors around them. [17] The most shocking case about sexual violence against women occurred in the Indonesian Riot of May 1988 when hundreds or even thousands of Chinese women were raped in a chaos situation of political reformation era in Indonesia. Rooted from this incident, the National Women Committee of Indonesia or *Komnas Perempuan* was established on October 15, 1998.

According to this human rights organisation, the Indonesian government has made efforts in addressing the rights, needs and protection of women through policies that have been issued. Indonesia has ratified the CEDAW into Law No. 7 of 1984, Law No. 23 of 2004 on the Abolition of Domestic Violence, Law No. 21 of 2007 on Eradication of Human Trafficking, and Law No. 36 of 2009 on Health. Derivatives of each law is one of the mandates of the government—in this case the Ministry of Women's Empowerment and Child Protection—to construct a minimum service standard and standard operating procedures (SOPs) which will serve as guidelines in the implementation of integrated services for women and children who have been victims of violence by the relevant ministries and agencies. [18]

The punishment for any rape towards a child has also been arranged in Laws 81 and 82 with the minimum punishment of three years until twelve years. However, comparing to the long-term effects resulting from VAW, the law that arranges for the punishment as well as mechanism to punish the actors and to protect and give appropriate treatment to victims is somehow not enough.

Violence against Women in India

Based on the report compiled from the Human Rights Watch, India made crucial headlines regarding VAW. For example, in 2012, the case of Delhi gang rape and murder shocked the nation, forcing the prosecutors to use death penalty. In August last year, village leaders in Uttar Pradesh allegedly ordered rape of two Dalit sisters to pay for the "sins" of their brother who had eloped with a higher-caste woman. [19]

The National Crime Record Bureau of India recorded that from 2010 to 2014, the number of crimes against women dramatically increased. In 2010, the total number of crimes against women was pegged at 2,05,009 and in 2014, this number rose to 3,25,329. From these numbers, in 2010, most cases were dominated of cruelty by husband or his relatives (94,041), assault on women with intent to outrage her modesty (40,613), kidnapping and abduction (29,795), and rape (22,172). Whereas in 2015, most criminal against women cases were dominated with cruelty by husband or his relatives (1,22,877), assault on women with intent to outrage her modesty (82,235), kidnapping and abduction (57,311), and rape (36,735). Further, according to the Report, the rate of crime against women in India during 2014 was mostly found in the states of Rajasthan and Assam at an alarmingly above 90 percent. [20]

Opposing most assumptions about crime against women in India, rape is not the most found case. In 2015, there had been a reduction in rape cases compared to 2014 by 5.7 percent, coming down from 36,735 to 34,651. [21]

However, rape cases, especially the gang rapes, became the most highlighted cases for crime against women in India. In 2014, gang rape cases totalled 2,346 and showed a decline in 2015 with as many as 2,113 cases being reported. Further, in 2015, from 34,651 rape cases, 33,098 cases were afflicted by offenders known to the victim, especially on the promise of marriage (23.12 percent) and other known persons to the victim (34.76 percent). In Assam and Bihar states, there had been more than 90 percent cases of rape done by unknown offenders. Half of the rape cases in India involved women between ages 18 to 29. However, if the rape cases were compared based on the numbers of incidents, Delhi had the worst rates with a total number of 2,199 cases reported. [22]

Women's Rights and Security in Asia Region: What Will Be Next?

ASEAN's concern in human rights issues as it is found in the ASEAN Human Rights Declaration has at least given a good sign on the progress of ASEAN's vision to protect all of its member states in an equal way. Especially for enhancing the women's rights, ASEAN has also committed itself to elevate Southeast Asian women from poverty so that they can actively participate in economic transformation. Nevertheless, there are still some weakness aspects that need to be upgraded in order to prove ASEAN's commitment on women's rights. With the establishment of these regional human rights institutions, ASEAN has indeed conveyed that development in the region cannot be measured solely through economic numbers, but progress must also be based on good governance, inclusivity, and protection of human rights with priority on women's rights being included in this respect. These institutions also signal to strategic partners and neighbours that individual ASEAN member states expect international relations to be conducted according to international rules and standards. Another factor is that, this ASEAN concern of human rights agenda also influences how territorial and economic disputes are resolved, along with the enhancement of trade and other ties. [23]

India also shares a similar concern and awareness towards VAW. Sexual harassment, along with child abuse is obviously a cause for concern in India, particularly after the brutal attack on a young woman who was gang raped and killed on a bus in New Delhi. Condemnation and protests were widespread across the nation and global countries. The Indian Parliament responded to the critics by installing panic buttons and other emergency devices on buses to inform the police in case of potential sexual violence. In addition, the country has also issued another regulation requiring all mobile phones sold in country from 2017 to include a panic button and from 2018 onwards, phones will be also set to include GPS navigation systems. [24]

The United Nations has noted that there are at least four cultural aspects that might be important for ASEAN and India to recognize regarding the protection from crime and violence against women, as enumerated below: [25]

1. Inadequate legal frameworks addressing VAW.
2. Pervasive impunity for violence against women in the region due to lack of gender-sensitivity and gender-responsiveness in law enforcement, and the formal, semi-formal, parallel justice and alternative dispute resolution systems.
3. Large numbers of unreported cases of VAW due to limited awareness of existing laws, poor law enforcement, lack of support services to survivors such as health care, legal aid, and psycho-social counselling.
4. Poor implementation of existing laws due to limited understanding and capacity of law enforcers, judiciary, local government, health care sector and others involved.

In overall analysis, legal frameworks in ASEAN member states still possesses gaps in complying with the CEDAW norms of non-discrimination and substantive equality. Laws in ASEAN member states, like, for example, in Indonesia, often reinforce socially constructed and stereotyped roles of men and women in the family, community and society. Most of the domestic legislations are dominated with the notion of the superiority of men over women and similarly construed notions of women's sexuality and of masculinity. The United

Nations observed that, for example, in Cambodia and Thailand, the definition of domestic violence exclude acts of disciplining wives if it is conducted with "compassion" or because of "negligence".

In Brunei, Lao PDR, and also Vietnam, a number of legal provisions allow marital rape or simply do not recognize it as a crime. Also, generally, women do not receive remedies for violations of their rights. They are discouraged to pursue justice by the inadequate systems and structures that fail to meet needs of the survivors of VAW. In Indonesia, for example, as the most dominant culture is coming from the Javanese, the Javanese cultures towards family and pride dominates the society image of VAW. In particular, sexual violence cases are often settled out of court by parents of the survivors by receiving the compensation. In some cases, women are even forced to marry the perpetrators to protect family honour. Furthermore, in most of Southeast Asian nations, and particularly in Indonesia, women often have limited access to justice because they lack economic resources or mobility to reach justice and support services. [26]

In India, rape cases are still highly under reported. Indian society is still marred by concerns about stigma that surrounds sexual crimes and resultantly many cases go unreported. Even to report and discuss such crimes is considered a "taboo". Although VAW is not unique to India, but the nation still believes in cultural practices that undermine women's role in the society. Most of the Indian society still holds traditional beliefs such as preference for a male child, making females vulnerable to violence and discrimination. Due to high demands for change from feminist groups, led by 35 women organizations, student activist groups, and trade unions to form a coalition called Dahej Virodhi Chetna Manch (DVCM), recent legislative and judicial measures are now addressing more issues of women protection from crimes and sexual violence. However, the political will to decrease VAW in India is still low, and also, court battles and judges still cite personal religious bias to intervene in family matters. [27]

Thus, it can be said that within the Asian region, the term of women's rights are still hard to fully implement due to many factors as have been described before. ASEAN Charter that promotes the existence of human rights has mentioned no descriptive explanation about mechanism to achieve women's rights. Furthermore, the documents of ASEAN Human's Rights Declaration cannot also measure any policies to solve VAW in ASEAN member states. ASEAN still recognizes VAW as a soft issue and due to the non-interference principle that each ASEAN member states hold, they are less likely to compromise on women's issues as a common threat issue. In order to completely secure women's rights, ASEAN members must collect political will from each member state and regional instruments of legal law should be established. A body should be enabled to decide whether a state has failed to comply with women's rights provisions under the purview of international human rights standards. The international law regarding women's rights can be established as the first prior reference for the regional laws related to the mechanism of preventing and dealing with VAW in the Asian region. [28]

Conclusion

In the Asian region, women's rights issues are still considered as a soft problem and thus the policy to cope with VAW still heavily depends on each nation's local laws. ASEAN as one formal institution should unite ten Southeast Asian countries under one regionalism that should be committed in coping human rights problem as is outlined in the ASEAN Charter [Articles 1.7, 2.2(i) and 14] and other important ASEAN documents. ASEAN also established AICHR in 2009 and it was followed by ASEAN Declaration of Human Rights in 2012 as one tangible action from ASEAN regarding issues of human rights. These human rights issues that ASEAN took up was actually derived from the international human rights concept that emerged for the first time in national documents such as Magna Carta (1215), the Petition of Rights (1628), and the Bill of Rights (1689) in England, to be followed by many other declarations on human rights. For this reason, ASEAN surely has an obligation to force the establishment of human rights for all Southeast Asian people equally.

In Indonesia and India, VAW has been a major problem for the women and the number of VAW cases has been gradually increasing each year with the most common VAW related to sexual violence. Indonesian and Indian laws that are related to the punishment of VAW offenders are both considered to be weak. By strengthening the commitment in accomplishing equal human rights, the implementation of laws related to VAW cases in Indonesia and India should be further strengthened and enforced fairly.

Endnotes

1. Fanny M. Cheung et al. (1999) (ed.), "Breaking the Silence: Violence against Women in Asia", UNESCO National Commission of the Philippines, pp.1-2.
2. The United Nations Women for Southeast Asia official documents, UN Women Issue Briefs on Women's Human Rights in the ASEAN Region: Violence Against Women, available at: http://cedaw-seasia.org/docs/issue_brief/IssueBrief_Violence%20Against%20Women.pdf.
3. World Health Organization's (WHO) official websites, "Violence against Women: Definition and Scope of the Problem", July 2007, available at: http://www.who.int/gender/violence/v4.pdf.
4. Patricia Tjaden (2005), "Defining and Measuring Violence against Women: Background, Issues, and Recommendations", Expert Group Meeting, Organized by UN Division for the Advancement of Women in collaboration with: Economic Commission for Europe (ECE) and World Health Organization (WHO)11-14 April, Geneva Switzerland, available at: http://www.un.org/womenwatch/daw/egm/vaw-stat-2005/docs/expert-papers/Tjaden.pdf.
5. BBC News for Indonesia (2012), "Violence against Women in

Indonesia", available at: http://www.bbc.co.uk/indonesia/berita_indonesia/2012/03/120307_komnasperempuan.shtml.

6. The United Nations Women official websites (2012), "Declarations, Reservations and Objections to CEDAW", available at: http://www.un.org/womenwatch/daw/cedaw/reservations-country.htm.
7. The Global Network of Women Peace Builder official websites, available at: http://www.gnwp.org/written-statement-submitted-to-cedaw-on-the-occasion-of-the-general-discussion-on-women-in-conflict-and-post-conflict-situations.
8. The United Nations Women for Southeast Asia official documents, UN Women Issue Briefs on Women's Human Rights in the ASEAN Region: Violence against Women, available at: http://cedaw-seasia.org/docs/issue_brief/Issue_Brief_Violence%20Against%20Women.pdf.
9. Hortreiter, op. cit., pp. 32-76.
10. Hanumanthappa, 2015, p. 475.
11. Edugeneral, 2016.
12. Yunus and Varma, 2015, pp. 368-369.
13. Saarinah Sadli and Tita Marlita (2012), "Violence against Women in Indonesia", in 'Breaking the Silent: Violence against Women in Asia', Fanny M. Cheung (ed.), UNESCO National Commission of the Philippines, p. 82.
14. WHO, op. cit, p. 3.
15. WHO, op. cit., p. 2.
16. United Nations of Women, op. cit, pp. 3-4.
17. available at: http://us.log.viva.co.id/news/read/190382-11-kekerasan-seksual-terhadap-perempuan.
18. Ikatan Perempuan Positif Indonesia, Pendokumentasian Kekerasan Terhadap Perempuan Dengan HIV (2012), available at: http://www.ippi.or.id/wp-content/uploads/2012/11/Laporan-Survey-Kekerasan-IPPI-20121.pdf.
19. Human Rights Watch (2016), available at: https://www.hrw.org/world-report/2016/country-

chapters/india#d91ede.

20. The National Crime Record Bureau of India (2014), "Crime in India".
21. Salve (2016), "Crimes Reports in India".
22. *The Indian Express*, September 1, 2015.
23. Katherine G. Southwick (2013), "Bumpy Road to ASEAN Human's Rights Declaration", Asia Pacific Bulletin No. 197, January 22, *East West Centre Journal*, p. 1.
24. *Al Jazeera News*, (ed.), September 1, 2016.
25. United Nations for Women, op. cit., pp. 4-6.
26. United Nations for Women, op. cit., p. 6.
27. Kethineni (2017), "VAW in India: Legislative and Policy Reforms".
28. Mahmudin Nur Al-Gozaly (2012), "Whither Women's Rights in ASEAN?", December 4, available at: http://www.thejakartapost.com/news/2012/12/04/whither-women-s-rights-asean.html.

References

Al Jazeera News (2016), "Rape Reported Cases in India", available at: http://www.aljazeera.com/news/2016/08/india-34000-cases-rape-reported-2015-160831140518208.html.

Cheung, Fanny M. et al. (1999), (ed.), "Breaking the Silence: Violence against Women in Asia", UNESCO National Commission of the Philippines, Manila.

Fified, Russell H. (1979), "National and Regional Interest in ASEAN Competition and Cooperation in International Politics", Occasional Paper, No. 57, ISEAS, Singapore.

Gyngell, Allan (1983), "Looking Outwards: ASEAN's External Relations", in Alison Broinowski (ed.), 'Understanding ASEAN', Macmillan Press Ltd., London.

Hortreiter, Isabel (2001), "Women's Human Rights in Southeast Asia", Friedrich Ebert Stiftung (FES), Bangkok.

International Council on Social Welfare (2001), "Civil Society and ASEAN", ICSW Printing Press, Bangkok.

Kethineni, Sesha (2017), "VAW in India: Legislative and Policy Reforms", *Georgetown Journal of International Affairs*, available at: http://journal.georgetown.edu/violence-against-women-in-india-legislative-and-policy-reforms.

Mohammed, Nasrudin (2005), "ASEAN and Administration: Regional Threats", *Pemikir*, No. 41, July-September, Malaysia.

Sadli, Saarinah and Tita Marlita (2012), "Violence against Women in Indonesia", in Fanny M. Cheung (ed.), 'Breaking the Silent: Violence Against Women in Asia', UNESCO National Commission of the Philippines, Manila.

Solidium, Estrella D. (2003), "The Politics of ASEAN: An Introduction to Southeast Asian Regionalism", Eastern Universities Press, Singapore.

Southwick, Katherine G. (2013), "Bumpy Road to ASEAN Human's Rights Declaration", *Asia Pacific Bulletin*, No. 197, January 22, East West Centre, US.

3

ASEAN-India Free Trade Agreement: Reducing Non-tariff Trade Cost

Rajan Sudesh Ratna and Jing Huang

Abstract

The formations of free trade agreements (FTAs) are changing international trade, especially in terms of reduction and removal of tariff and non-tariff barriers. The ASEAN-India Free Trade Agreement (AIFTA) emerged from a mutual interest of both parties to expand their economic ties in the Asia-Pacific region. India's 'Look East Policy' was reciprocated by similar interests of many ASEAN countries to expand their interactions westward. There is a big gain for India and ASEAN countries, in particular after the entry of AIFTA into force—the total bilateral trade increased more than threefold from US$ 21 billion in 2005-2006 to US$ 65 billion in 2015-2016.

India and ASEAN countries' economy are the most energetic ones in the Asia-Pacific region. Scholars have done a lot of researches to help improve this agreement become more comprehensive. However those researches do not have any studies focussed on its tariff and non-tariff measure issues. Therefore in this paper, we are using the gravity model and evaluating the impact of elimination of non-tariff related trade cost on AIFTA exports keeping in view the future negotiations prospects. As evaluated, nowadays, NTMs are becoming much stronger determination factors in bilateral trade than the traditional tariff barrier measures which could restrict market access. The NTMs represent a challenge for exporters as well as importers and could raise the price of goods traded.

ASEAN has been a pivot in developing RTAs in the Asia-Pacific region attempting to create itself as a 'hub' for regionalism. Despite the significant achievement of developing RTAs in the region, economic liberalization has not been fully accomplished due to different provisions applied among the RTAs. This situation creates a "noodle-bowl" effect, which further increases costs of trade within blocks and possibly decreases the opportunities for new trade and investments.

India is one of the most active nations on trade front in the Asia-Pacific region. Going by the record at WTO, India had notified 15 RTAs to WTO by end-2015. India's tariff liberalisation in its RTAs tends to vary greatly depending on the negotiating partner. India's tariff liberalisation commitments with ASEAN are 75 percent of its tariff line for imports from the ASEAN countries.

Under AIFTA, during 2004-2015, India-ASEAN exports grew faster (approximately at a rate of 16.2 percent) compared to export growth of 10.6 percent for the rest of the world. Among the ASEAN member countries, Singapore enjoyed the highest amount of trade with India. Up to 2015, India became the seventh largest export market for ASEAN.

Tariff Profiles of RCEP Countries

The current import duties (commoly known as MFN or applied rate of duties) are much lower than the bound rates agreed in the Uruguay Round (to be brought to the bound levels during 2000-2005) which is due to autonomous liberalisation by many countries. The commitments to bring applied duties down to zero due to FTAs is also one of the reasons for autonomous liberalisation as countries realise the benefit of liberalisation and are also confident that their industries can face the challenges and would become globally competitive. Due to this, in most of the items, there exists a large gap between the bound rates and MFN duties, especially in case of developing countries. The gap is likely to be narrowed down after the conclusion of the Doha round negotiations. The negotiations to tariff elimination in FTAs are held on the basis of applied tariffs which are different than the apporach taken in GATT/WTO which uses bound rates as the benchmark.

Among ASEAN countries, Myanmar has the highest average bound tariff rate (83.4 percent), followed by India (48.7 percent) and Indonesia (37.1 percent). In terms of applied tariff rate, India shows the highest rate (12.6 percent), followed by Republic of Korea (12.1 percent), Cambodia (10.9 percent) and Lao PDR (9.7 percent), while Singapore follows a duty free MFN tariff, even though has a bound rate of 10 percent. However, these countries have already brought their duties to zero in ASEAN FTAs.

Non-tariff Measures (NTMs)

Non-tariff measures are not easy to define and are interchangeable with the term non-tariff barriers. As the term suggests, NTMs are broadly defined as any policy measure other than customs tariffs that can have an influence on international trade flow. According to UNCTAD (2012), NTMs on import side can be categorized into two groups: technical measures and non-technical measures.

Technical Measures: These are as under:

Sanitary and Phytosanitary (SPS) Measures: SPS measures are defined as any measure applied to protect human or animal life from risks arising from additives, contaminations, toxins or disease causing organisms in their food, to protect human life from plant or animal carried diseases, to protect animal or plant life from pests, diseases or disease causing organisms and to prevent or limit other damage to a country from entry, establishment or spread of diseases.

Technical Barriers to Trade (TBTs): TBT measures include technical regulations, standards and conformity assessment procedures (WTO, 2004). TBT measures typically deal with labelling of composition or quality of food, drink or drugs, quality requirements for fresh food, volume, shape and appearance of packaging etc.

Non-technical Measures: These are as follows:

Quotas: Restriction of imports of specified products by setting a maximum quantity or value of goods authorized for import.

Non-automatic Licensing: Non-automatic licensing is usually the means for administering a quota or a conditional prohibition and in such cases is a condition for import.

Voluntary Export Restraints (VERs): Voluntary export restraints (VERs) are usually informal export restraint arrangements (ERAs) between an exporter and an importer whereby the exporter agrees to limit the exports for a certain period of time.

Prohibitions: Unconditional interdiction to import. The so-called "prohibition with exceptions" is incorporated in the category of licensing which is relevant to the nature of the exception.

Anti-dumping Measures: Anti-dumping measures may be taken after an investigation by the investigating authority of the importing country has led to a determination of dumping and material injury resulting there from. It is considered that dumping takes place when a product is introduced into the commerce of an importing country at less than its normal value

Countervailing Measures: Countervailing measures may be taken after an investigation by the investigating authority of the importing country has led to a determination that the imported goods are benefiting from subsidies, and that they result in injury. Countervailing measures may take the form of countervailing duties or undertakings by the exporting firms or by the authorities of the subsidizing country.

Government Procurement Procedures: Government procurement procedures typically involve a price preference for domestic goods. The price preference is computed to determine the outcome of public tenders for the supply of goods or services to government agencies.

Certain types of NTMs have been dealt in the multilateral

trading system. During the early GATT negotiating rounds, the members recognized that NTMs can distort the impact of significant tariff reduction and in the Kennedy Round (1964-1967), members agreed to deal with NTMs in the forthcoming negotiations.

The Tokyo Round (1973-1979) created a special negotiating sub-committee on technical barriers, customs, subsidies and countervailing measures, and government procurement. In the Uruguay Rounds, comprehensive negotiations led to disciplining some NTMs like import licensing, quota, standards and technical regulations, rules of origin etc.

The agreements on Sanitary and Phytosanitary measures (SPS), Technical Barriers to Trade (TBT) and others came into force on January 1, 1995. The Doha Round is also discussing further disciplining some of the issues relating to NTMs and the Trade Facilitation Agreement agreed in Bali Ministerial meeting in December 2013 is one such decision. The GATT rules on NTMs, however, are 'generally consistent with a shallow integration approach' (WTO, 2012).

As discussed earlier, in view of the reduced tariffs mostly due to autonomous liberalization, the important barriers to trade now are the non-tariff ones at the border as well as behind the border. Though certain non-tariff measures (export and import quotas, import licenses, monopoly trade measures etc.) have been disciplined under WTO, still a significant amount of non-tariff measures remain. Despite having disciplines on SPS and TBT in WTO, their use is increasing day by day. Costs associated of complying with these regulatory procedures are impacting trade. ESCAP (2011) has estimated the tariff and non-tariff trade costs and found that non-tariff trade costs are higher than the tariff trade cost. WTO (2012) observed that TBT/SPS measures distort trade in agricultural products. It would thus be important to look at non-tariff related trade cost of RCEP members and examine whether reduction of trade cost is possible through the instruments of harmonisation, mutual recognition, equivalence, conformity assessment etc.

Recent studies on RCEP have stressed the importance of addressing NTMs. They proposed that priority should be given to address NTMs from the beginning of negotiations and RCEP must develop standards to measure NTMs and provide common approaches and conformity assessments (Das, 2012). It has also been pointed out that RCEP should clarify the types of NTMs to avoid delay of elimination of it due to lack of clear definition and they should be removed as much as possible (ERIA, 2013). Since the text of negotiation is not available in the public domain, it is also not known if initiatives taken by ASEAN to address NTMs, mostly through the process of harmonisation is also being discussed in RCEP or not. However, for a successful market access it is necessary that these additional costs associated with the NTMs are addressed in RCEP negotiations, importance of which is discussed in the following section.

Overall trade restrictiveness index (OTRI) summarizes the trade policy stance of a country by calculating the uniform tariff rate (replacing current tariff schedule and NTMs) that will keep its overall imports at the current level. OTRI is a more sophisticated way to calculate the weighted average tariff of a given country. The weights indicate the composition of import volume and import demand elasticities of each imported product. The empirical methodology of the OTRI was first developed in Kee, Nicita and Olarreaga (2008, 2009), based on the theoretical underpinning of Anderson and Neary (1994, 1996, 2003). NTMs considered in this calculation include price control measures, quantitative restrictions, monopolistic measures, technical regulations, and agriculture support.

Quantifying NTMs

The analytical studies show that NTMs play a significant role in trade restrictiveness. The fact that NTMs especially in terms of SPS and TBT standards vary greatly across countries, makes harmonization of standards a policy priority. Basic economic theory explains that if standards are necessary (e.g. for food safety), then commonly agreed international standards should facilitate trade by harmonizing the production process for all countries. In practice, the harmonization should remove trade restrictions, as production processes do not need to be customized to meet requirements for each export market. SPS and TBT standards and regulations are double-edged swords. On one hand, SPS and TBT measures can promote economic development and trade and on the other hand, they may also be used as disguised protectionism and unnecessarily frustrate international trade. The risk of the use of these measures for protecting the domestic producers is particularly high in the agriculture sector where lowering the level of protection provided by tariff, increases the importance of sanitary and phytosanitary measures as border protection instruments. The major difficulty in dealing with standards and regulations is to distinguish those measures which are justified by a legitimate cause from those which are applied for protectionists' purposes (Ratna, 2005).

The studies on harmonization generally compare country-specific standards to internationally set guidelines. Sithamaparam and Devadason (2011), for example, assessed the impact of NTMs on Malaysian exports by examining the heterogeneity of various export markets (European Union, Japan and ASEAN-4). They also found a positive effect of harmonization of standards. Their results suggest that, while exports to ASEAN-4 have increased because of the harmonization of regional standards, they have not increased to the European Union, which generally adopts different standards for other regions.

Wilson, Otsuki and Majumdar (2003) examined the impact of antibiotic residue standards on trade in beef and analysed the trade effect of setting harmonized international standards. They specifically looked at the diverse standards applied in six importing countries or regions (Australia, New Zealand, United States, Canada, European Union and Japan) and how these affected exports from a number of countries (Australia,

Argentina, Brazil, Canada, Chile, China, Hungary, Mexico, New Zealand, Nicaragua, South Africa, Switzerland, Thailand, Ukraine, Uruguay and United States). By using an econometric approach, the study found that bovine meat imports are significantly lower for an importing country that has a more stringent standard on an antibiotic item.

They also found that not all countries would benefit from such harmonization. While a universally adopted Codex standard on beef would significantly increase bovine meat exports from the emerging developing countries, it would decrease exports from low-income countries. The reason is that many low-income countries can export only to countries applying relatively lax standards as they do not have production processes in line with the Codex standards, let alone the more stringent standards prescribed by many high-income markets.

The diverse trade impact from standard harmonization based on country's development level is also found in the study by Cadot et al. (2010). The study shows that the existence of PTAs between developed and developing countries (North-South agreements) hurts trade between developing countries (South-South trade) and impedes developing countries' attempts to diversify into new markets if such harmonisation is on regional standards. Chen and Mattoo (2008) estimated a gravity model of bilateral trade of 28 OECD countries and 14 non-OECD countries at the three-digit SITC product level. They found that harmonization agreements can increase trade between participating countries but will not necessarily increase trade with other countries. In particular, they found that harmonization increases exports from developed countries outside the region, but it reduces exports from developing countries within the region.

MRAs tend to increase trade within the region. MRAs also increase trade with countries outside the region if they are not associated with rules of origin. However, when the MRAs contain rules of origin, trade with countries outside the region is negatively affected, especially exports from developing countries. Overall, the evidence suggests that regional integration of TBT/SPS measures has trade-diverting effects, especially to the detriment of developing countries. This finding is consistent with the evidence that deep preferential trade agreements in the area of TBT/SPS measures are more likely among countries with a higher and more similar level of income. This finding also highlights the risk that regional integration on TBT/SPS measures may lead to a multi-tiered world where certain developing countries are marginalized.

Furthermore, as stressed in World Trade Report, 2011, there is a risk of a "lock-in" effect, whereby the regional harmonization of standards may reduce incentives for further trade opening. Regardless of their objective, TBT/SPS measures may or may not reduce trade. Negative trade effects, when they exist, generate negative spillovers across countries. This provides a rationale for international co-operation. Harmonization and mutual recognition help to reduce the undesired negative trade effects of legitimate public policy. However, both approaches highlight the need for capacity building to address regulatory challenges in developing countries. The costs related to compliance and conformity assessment impinge, particularly on developing countries. This is because they lack the technical infrastructure necessary to effectively develop and design technical regulations, standards and conformity assessment procedures.

Given the increasing importance of NTMs, researchers have also used the gravity model to estimate the impact of NTMs on trade. The gravity model has been used to examine bilateral trade flows, particularly to estimate the impacts of trade-related policies on the trade flows.

The basic gravity model can be written as:

$$Log\ (Trade\ flow_{ij}) = b_0 + b_1 log(GDP_i) + b_2 log(GDP_j) + b_3 log\ (Distance_{ij}) + e_{ij} \quad \ldots\ldots(1)$$

Gravity based techniques measure the trade impact of NTMs rather than their welfare effect and thus ignore some of the effects of regulations that correct market failures but restrict trade. It also captures the trade enhancing effects of regulations when they act as standards that facilitate trade (Beghnin and Bureau, 2001).

The effect of TBT on trade impact was studied for twelve western European nations from 1980-1995 and the study helped in estimating impact of 1 percent increase in the number of shared standards on bilateral trade flows (Moenius, 2004). Hoekman and Nicita (2008) did a study to analyse the impact of trade policies on developing countries. The data set covered 104 importers and 115 exporters. The study used a traditional cross-section gravity model that dealt with trade volume as dependent variable, and multilateral resistance terms (distance, language, landlocked, adjacency), trade policies (TTRI, NTM) and domestic trade costs as explanatory variables. The analysis in the paper suggested that tariff and NTMs are statistically significant determinants of trade flow. On an average, 10 percent of TTRI reduction would increase trade volumes by approximately 2 percent, while NTMs add another 1.8 percent. Furthermore, the study showed the importance of other trade costs such as transactions costs at and behind the border as well, especially for low-income countries.

Bellanawithana et al. (2009) examined the effect of NTM on agricultural exports using the gravity model approach by using the value of agriculture trade flows as dependent variable and used the gravity model variables like GDP, distance, geographical proximity like common border, landlocked country and other variables like common language, colonial ties etc. The trade restrictiveness indices of TTRI and OTRI were used as constructed by Kee, Nicita and Olarreage (2006). The regression analysis presented that NTM has significant negative effect on south-south and north-south trade, while NTM has insignificant effect on agricultural exports in south-north and north-north trade.

Methodology and Limitations of the Model

This section aims to quantify the impacts of NTMs on overall market access, particularly for all products between India and ASEAN member countries. This section evaluates if the elimination of tariffs under the AIFTA would be sufficient for enhanced market access or addressing the issues of NTMs would be equally important, if not more. The biggest challenge for researchers to study impact of NTMs on trade is to find exclusive non-tariff measures as per WTO or UNCTAD classifications at product level and then to express them in tariff equivalent form so that it could be used in the model. Various databases that quantify NTM like TRAINS or ESCAP-World Bank trade cost database are at aggregate level and not at the 6 or 8 digit product level (HS) classification, hence a sectoral (at 2 digit HS level) or product (6 or 8 digit HS level) based analysis is very difficult. In this study, the trade restrictiveness indices have been used from ESCAP-World Bank trade cost database—bilateral tariff cost and non-tariff equivalent trade costs. The ESCAP-World Bank trade cost database is comprehensive as it includes all costs involved in international trade of goods.

In order to derive the relationships between tariffs, NTMs and FTA on trade flows respectively, the gravity model has been used to examine the relationship between bilateral trade flows by using standard gravity variables and bilateral trade cost relating to NTMs. The factors are known to have an influence on trade and that have also been used in this model are importing countries GDP, exporting countries GDP, distance, language, common border, landlocked geographical position and colonial legacy. The standard gravity model has been used as a first model (Model 1) to analyse this relationship for RCEP members. In the second model (Model 2), FTA variable has been added to test the assumption that FTA enhances trade among FTA partner countries and thus export will have a positive and statistically significant relation with FTA.

Model 2 thus examines the relationship between exports and FTA. The third model (Model 3) is an improved version of Model 2 where two more factors, TTC (bilateral tariff trade cost) and NTTC (non-tariff trade cost) have been added. In the third model (Model 3), the impact of TTC and NTTC on the exports was examined first by having the FTA variable (Model 3a) and then by dropping the FTA variable (Model 3b). From these three models, one tries to examine which factor is the most influential in affecting intra-RCEP exports—will trade increase if in the FTA only the tariff issues are addressed (by bringing them to zero) or there is a need to address the non-tariff issues simultaneously in the negotiations.

The gravity model can be represented by the following equations for the above mentioned three models:

Model 1:

$$\ln(v)_{ijt} = b_0 + b_1 ln(GDP)_{it} + b_2 ln(GDP)_{jt} + b_3 \ln(Dist)_{ij} + b_4(Lang)_{ij} + b_5(Conting)_{ij} + b_6(Landlock)_j + b_7(Colony)_{ij} + e_{ij} \quad \ldots\ldots(2)$$

Model 2:

$$\ln(v)_{ijt} = b_0 + b_1 ln(GDP)_{it} + b_2 ln(GDP)_{jt} + b_3 \ln(Dist)_{ij} + b_4(Lang)_{ij} + b_5(Conting)_{ij} + b_6(Landlock)_j + b_7(Colony)_{ij} + b_8(FTA)_{ijt} + e_{ij} \quad \ldots\ldots(3)$$

Model 3:

$$\ln(v)_{ijt} = b_0 + b_1 ln(GDP)_{it} + b_2 ln(GDP)_{jt} + b_3 \ln(Dist)_{ij} + b_4(Lang)_{ij} + b_5(Conting)_{ij} + b_6(Landlock)_j + b_7(Colony)_{ij} + b_8(FTA)_{ijt} + b_9(TTC)_{ijt} + b_{10}(NTTC)_{ijt} + e_{ij} \quad \ldots\ldots(4)$$

Where "b" terms are co-efficients, "i" is the importer and "j" is the exporter. The explanation for each independent variable is as below:

v_{ijt}: value of exports from country j to country i at year t

Basic Gravity Variables

GDP_{it}: GDP in the ith importer at year t

GDP_{jt}: GDP in the jth exporter at year t

$Dist_{ij}$: geographical distance between capital cities in i and j

Trade Restrictiveness Indices

TTCijt: bilateral tariff trade cost imposed by importer i when exported by exporter j at year t

NTTCijt: non-tariff trade cost component imposed by importer i when exported by exporter j at year t

FTA_{itj}: 1 if ith importer has free trade agreement in force with country j, dummy variable

Cultural Variables

$Lang_{ij}$: 1 if both countries share the same official language, dummy variable

$Colony_{ij}$: 1 if ith importer has colony ties with jth exporter, dummy variable

Geographical Variables

$Conting_{ij}$: 1 if country i share a land border with country j, dummy variable

$Landlock_{j}$: 1 if jth exporter is a landlocked country, dummy variable

e_{ij}: error term

The data set covers India and its 10 ASEAN trading countries for the data years between 1995 and 2011. The data from 1995 was taken as it captures the impact of effective tariff reduction due to Uruguay Round results (from 1995 to 2000, with flexibility to developing countries), autonomous tariff liberalisation taken during the period and the fact that the phenomena of FTAs in Asia and the Pacific started in a big way from 2002-2003. The latest trade cost database is available only up to 2011. The detailed information on the sources for data is given in Table 3.1.

The gravity model estimations were done using the statistical software package STATA/12.

Table 3.1: Variables and Sources

Variable	Source
v_{ijt}	UNCOMTRADE
GDP_{it}	World Bank, IMF
GDP_{jt}	World Bank, IMF
$Dist_{ij}$	CEPII
TTCij	Authors' calculation based on ESCAP-World Bank trade cost database
NTTCij	ESCAP- World Bank trade cost database
$Lang_{ij}$	CEPII
$Colony_{ij}$	CEPII
$Conting_{ij}$	CEPII
$Landlock_{j}$	CEPII
FTA_{ij}	APTIAD database, UNESCAP

Result and Discussion

The econometric estimations of equations (2), (3) and (4) are based on OLS, Fixed Effect (FE) and Random Effects (RE) technique. The RE can be preferred over FE in this kind of panel data setup because of the presence of time invariant explanatory variables like language, colony, FTA, landlocked in the model, however the FE is useful for addressing the endogeneity issue which often arises in gravity models when estimating the impact of trade policies, especially in RTAs. FE can help to overcome part of the endogeneity problem due to omitted variable bias, although time-varying omitted variables remain a problem. To get rid of the presence of heteroscedasticity, if any, the robust estimates were used in the models. Estimates for the gravity model were also attempted by using other popular regression methods like OLS, FE, Hausman-Taylor (HT) and Poisson Pseudo-Maximum Likelihood Estimator (PPML) to check the consistency of the results. It turned out that the results achieved from the OLS, FE and RE models are similar to other regression models. Here the regression result of FE and RE results are presented for model 3 above and the regression results are given in Table 3.2.

Table 3.2: Results for RCEP

	OLS	
	Model 3a	Model 3b
lngdp_importer	0.735***	0.730***
	(37.81)	(36.55)
lngdp_exporter	0.627***	0.621***
	(38.27)	(39.63)
ln_dist	-0.447***	-0.473***
	(-12.56)	(-15.48)
Lang	0.276***	0.279***
	(4.95)	(4.98)
Conting	-0.117	-0.108
	(-1.61)	(-1.51)
Landlock	-1.332***	-1.337***
	(-8.01)	(-8.10)
Colony	-0.0219	-0.0408
	(-0.26)	(-0.49)
FTA	0.100	
	(1.64)	
TTC	-0.0378***	-0.0390***
	(-16.71)	(-19.10)
NTTC	-0.0167***	-0.0166***
	(-20.53)	(-20.94)
_cons	-4.462***	-3.980***
	(-8.32)	(-8.32)
N	2461	2461
	FE	
	Model 3a	Model 3b
lngdp_importer	0.573***	0.584***
	(13.36)	(13.69)
lngdp_exporter	0.687***	0.704***
	(15.62)	(16.26)
ln_dist	0.000623	-0.00405

Contd...

	(0.02)	(-0.12)
Lang	0.191	0.190
	(1.35)	(1.35)
Conting	0.0735	0.0732
	(0.22)	(0.22)
Landlock	0	0
	(.)	(.)
Colony	0.443	0.443
	(1.69)	(1.69)
FTA	0.0825*	
	(2.09)	
TTC	-0.0144***	-0.0145***
	(-8.99)	(-9.09)
NTTC	-0.0153***	-0.0154***
	(-28.25)	(-28.44)
_cons	-8.734***	-9.167***
	(-11.86)	(-12.97)
N	2461	2461

Contd...

	RE	
	Model 3a	Model 3b
lngdp_importer	0.736***	0.737***
	(14.36)	(4.96)
lngdp_exporter	0.618***	0.630***
	(14.79)	(15.04)
ln_dist	-0.0550	-0.0650
	(-1.02)	(-1.23)
Lang	0.202*	0.203*
	(2.12)	(2.12)
Conting	0.124	0.144
	(0.59)	(0.68)
Landlock	-1.725***	-1.667***
	(-4.26)	(-4.13)
Colony	0.436**	0.431**
	(2.76)	(2.76)
FTA	0.0905	
	(1.43)	

Contd...

TTC	-0.0168***	-0.0173***
	(-6.53)	(-6.65)
NTTC	-0.0157***	-0.0157***
	(-7.95)	(-7.95)
_cons	-7.637***	-7.879***
	(-6.30)	(-6.46)
N	2461	2461

t-statistics in parentheses; * p<0.05; ** p<0.01; *** p<0.001

The dependent variable is *ln* (natural logarithm) of actual exports and imports of AIFTA member countries. The first column shows the description of independent variables and the remaining columns show the coefficients that were obtained from the regression results for Models 3a and 3b. The positive and statistically significant relation of exports with the GDPs of importing and exporting country is as per the assumptions. Landlocked countries tend to trade less; especially in terms of exports (Hoekman and Nicita, 2008). In this model, it reflects this result. Distance is an important determinant of bilateral trade impacting the exports negatively, but results do not show it as statistically significant for AIFTA.

This possibly could be due to the fact that the members of AIFTA are not located geographically too far. Sharing common language is an important factor of bilateral trade as it facilitates trade due to better understanding of each others' documentations, procedures etc. However, the RE model shows that it has statistically significant impact on export at a 10 percent level. Sharing a common border variable is also an important determinant of bilateral trade, but it has no statistically significant impact in this model. The model shows different results for FE (not significant) and RE (significant at 5 percent level) on having common colonial relations among AIFTA members.

The FE results show that between FTA and exports there is a positive and significant relationship at 10 percent but not significant for RE. There could be two possible explanations for such behaviour. One explanation could be attributed to the fact that during the period 1995 to 2011, ASEAN FTA (zero duty regime) was in place; thus the impact of intra-ASEAN FTA exports were not captured in this model. Secondly, mostly ASEAN started after 2008 and is still going through the transition period of tariff liberalisation, thus the trade is not duty free during the period. Another reason which explains the insignificant relation, can be attributed to the decline in trade due to the global economic recession. The correlation with other variables is on expected lines.

This model illustrates statistically significant (at 1 percent level) and negative relationship between exports and the tariff and non-tariff trade cost in all three cases of OLS, FE and RE. It also brings out the fact that the impact of reduction of NTMs is equally important to the reduction in tariffs and thus it is important that AIFTA handles the non-tariff trade cost issues in the negotiations. In this regard, using the Model 3b, the impact assessment of NTTC was calculated by using the methodology adopted by ESCAP (2008). Using that methodology with RE coefficients, effort was made to predict the AIFTA export potential for the year 2011 (as the latest data was available only for 2011). In order to calculate the export potential, a hypothetical scenario was assumed where there is no existence of non-tariff trade cost i.e. the entire non-tariff trade cost is eliminated. This was done by taking the variable NTTC as zero and tried to find the estimated AIFTA export by using all the statistically significant variables in Model 3 as follows:

$$\text{Vijt} = -7.879 + 0.737 * (\text{GDP})_{it} + 0.630 * (\text{GDP})_{jt} + 0.203 * (\text{Lang})_{ij} - 1.667 * (\text{Landlock})_{j} + 0.431 * (\text{Colony})_{ij} - 0.0173 * (\text{TTC})_{ij} \quad \ldots\ldots(5)$$

This estimated gravity equation was then used to get the predicted export value of the AIFTA in 2011. The difference between the actual exports value and the predicted export value is considered as the "export potential" for the year 2011. A positive trade potential suggests that there is scope for an economy to increase its exports in RCEP with a particular trading partner during that period. It was found that if the NTTC is eliminated, it will generate an additional AIFTA exports to the tune of US$ 1,233 million which shows a growth of around 55 percent over the actual AIFTA export value of 2011 (US$ 2,253 million).

Conclusion

In this case, we examined the impact of tariff and non-tariff measures on AIFTA trade flows. The result of the analysis reveals some interesting points, even though there are certain limitations. The first being, not a very significant impact of FTA on trade expansion, which was found in this case. As pointed out, the lack of strong correlation could be due to ASEAN FTA which was in place during the period of analysis and ASEAN+1 agreements being in transition. The results, however, bring the greater importance of non-tariff measures on exports compared to the tariff barriers. Thus, the issues of non-tariff measures need to be adequately addressed in the AIFTA negotiations. Since the AIFTA members are also members to WTO, they are governed by the disciplines on NTMs especially on issues relating to SPS and TBT measures. However, given the nature of disputes that emerged in WTO on these issues as well as specific trade concerns, which have been raised in the meetings of SPS and TBT Committees, it is important that these are addressed in a time bound manner. One such initiative which has been taken at a regional level is the process of harmonisation of standards by ASEAN.

On the other side, the success will also depend on how strongly India and ASEAN integrate with the world economy. Unless high external protection levels are dismantled across the board, regional tariff liberalisation at the ASEAN-India level (or for that matter within the RCEP) could lead to substantial trade diversion.

References

Anderson, J.E. (1979), "A Theoretical Foundation for the Gravity Equation", *American Economic Review*, Vol. 69, pp. 106-116.

Anderson, James E. and J. Peter Neary (1994), "Measuring the Restrictiveness of Trade Policy," *World Bank Economic Review* 8(2), pp. 151-169.

Anderson, James and J. Peter Neary (1996), "A New Approach to Evaluating Trade Policy", *Review of Economic Studies* 63(1), pp. 107-125.

Anderson, James and J. Peter Neary (2003), "The Mercantilist Index of Trade Policy", *International Economic Review,* 44, pp. 627-649.

Anderson, J.E. and Van Wincoop E. (2001), "Gravity with Gravitas: A Solution to the Border Puzzle", NBER Working Paper 8079. Cambridge, MA.

Beguin, J.C., Bureau, J.C. (2001), "Quantitative Policy Analysis of Sanitary, Phytosanitary and Technical Barriers to Trade", *Economie Internationale*, Vol. 87, pp. 107-130.

Chen, M.X. and Mattoo, A. (2008), "Regionalism in Standards: Good or Bad for Trade?", *Canadian Journal of Economics*, 41(3), pp. 838-863.

Das, Sanchita Basu (2012), "RCEP: Going Beyond ASEAN+1 FTAs", ISEAS Perspective, August 17.

Deardorff, A.V. and Stern, R.M. (1998), "Measurement of Non-tariff Barriers", Studies in International Economics, The University of Michigan Press, Ann Harbour.

Debroy, B. (2005), "The SPS and TBT Agreements: Implications for Indian Policy", Working Paper No. 163, Indian Council for Research in International Economics Relations, New Delhi.

Herath, A. (2001), "Cost of Compliance of SPS Requirements in Beverages and Spices in Sri Lanka", paper contribution for International Workshop on Negotiating Agenda for Market Access, April 24-25, Geneva, Switzerland.

Hoekman, B. and Nicita, A. (2008), "Trade Policy, Trade Costs and Developing Country Trade", Policy Research Working Paper 4797, World Bank, Washington, DC.

Hummels, D. (2000), "Towards a Geography of Trade Costs", Working Paper, Purdue University.

Jayakody, P. (2006), "Non-tariff Barriers in North-South Trade: Sri Lanka's Country Perspective", Workshop on WTO Related Issues, May 2.

Kee, H.L., A. Nicita and M. Olarreaga (2006), "Estimating Trade Restrictiveness Indices", Trade Policy Research Working Paper

3840, World Bank, Washington, DC.

Kee, H.L., A. Nicita and M. Olarreaga (2008), "Import Demand Elasticities and Trade Distortions", *Review of Economics and Statistics*, Vol. 90, No. 4, pp. 666-682.

Kee, H.L., A. Nicita and M. Olarreaga (2009), "Estimating Trade Restrictiveness Indices", *Economic Journal*, Vol. 119, pp. 172-199.

Korinek, J., Melatos, M. and Marie-Luise Rau (2008), "A Review of Methods for Quantifying the Trade Effects of Standards in the Agri-food Sector", OECD Trade Policy Working Paper No. 79, OECD.

Laird, S. and Yeats, A. (1990), "Quantitative Methods for Trade-Barrier Analysis", Them Macmillan Press, London.

Maur, J.C. and Shepherd, B. (2011), "Product Standards", in Chauffour, J.P. and Maur, J.C. (eds.), 'Preferential Trade Policies for Trade Agreements: A Handbook', Washington DC, World Bank, pp. 197-216.

Mikic Mia and Wermelinger Martin (2010), "Rising Non-Tariff Protectionism and Crisis Recovery", ESCAP Document No. ST/ESCAP/2587.

Moenius, J. (2004), "Information versus Product Adaptation: The Role of Standards in Trade", International Business and Markets Research Centre Working Paper # 1, North-Western University.

Moenius, J. (2006), "The Good, the Bad and the Ambiguous: Standards and Trade in Agricultural Products", paper presented at the IATRC Summer Symposium 'Food Regulation and Trade: Institutional Framework, Concepts of Analysis and Empirical Evidence', Bonn, Germany, May 28-30.

Olper, A. and Raimondi, V. (2007), "Patterns and Determinants of International Trade cost in the Food Industry", paper presented at American Agricultural Economics Association Annual Meeting, Portland, July 29-August 1.

Peterson, E. and Orden, D. (2006), "Linking Risk and Economic Assessments in the Analysis of Plant Pest Regulations: The Case of US Imports of Mexican Avocados", electronic report from the Economic Research Service, US Department of Agriculture, October.

Ratna, Rajan Sudesh (2005), "The SPS Agreement: Indian Perspective" in Mehta, R. and George, J. (eds.), 'Food Safety Regulation Concerns and Trade: A Developing Country

Perspective', Macmillan India, pp. 73-98.

Saqib, M. and Taneja, N. (2005), "Non-tariff Barriers and India's Exports: The Case of ASEAN and Sri Lanka", working paper no. 165, Indian Council for Research on International Economic Relations, New Delhi.

UNCTAD/Commonwealth Secretariat (1996), "The Global Spice Trade and the Uruguay Round Agreements", UNCTAD, Geneva and Commonwealth Secretariat, London.

Weerasinghe, K.J. (2003), "Food Safety Issues: Trade and WTO Issues", Meeting the Changes in Developing Countries: An Asian Perspective", Agricultural Outlook Forum, February 20-21.

Wilson, J.S, Otsuki, T. and Majumdar, B. (2003), "Balancing Food Safety and Risk: Do Drug Residue Limits Affect International Trade in Beef?", *Journal of International Trade and Economic Development*, Vol. 12(4), pp. 377-402.

World Trade Organization (2011), "World Trade Report", Geneva.

World Trade Organization (2012), "World Trade Report", Geneva.

4

Education System in ASEAN and South Asia Region: A Comparison

Reni Juwitasari

Abstract

Human capital is an inseparable aspect of development and growth. Education is a tool and, at the same time, a milestone to empower human's capacities, resources, and opportunities. Yet, there have been many hitches towards the education system, burdening the will of changes to achieve development goals as stated in SDG's points, such as no poverty, quality of education, and gender equality. ASEAN as a regional organization has also coped up with education issues. There is still lack of participation from its citizens in terms of education. Considering the massive population, both India and Indonesia possess (as part of ASEAN countries), there are heavy challenges in implementing the three targets of sustainable development goals. Practically speaking, India and Indonesia have adopted an education system that is focused on vocational training to help both the countries in elevating development.

However, the targets have not yet been reached for all, particularly the girls. In Indonesia, there is less girl participation at the age of 10 until 19 (secondary high school), and more so in rural areas because of factors like early marriage, family economic condition, existence of high school facilities etc. Likewise, in India, girl participation rate has been decreasing in the age bracket of 15 until 19. In addition, less girl participation is also due to gender-stereotype that parents have against girls to get higher education. Thus, this paper aims to compare education system between India and Indonesia by using qualitative methods.

The data was sourced from government and NGO reports. The paper found that two countries are: (a) almost spending 3 percent of their GDP on education, (b) have a similar pattern of trilingual education, (c) emphasize on vocational courses, and (d) have a robust educational management system. Yet, they are facing challenges as regards gender-disparity in education caused by: (i) gender stereotype and (ii) the patriarchy system. This paper concludes that education plays an important role to empower people, especially the girl child and to elevate them for a better life, there is a need to break gender stereotype and patriarchy system in both the countries.

Introduction

A developing country obviously needs to develop human capital. Education being as a cornerstone of human development, it can empower people to maximize their capacities, resources and opportunities. [1] As a basic human right, education is meaningfully offered to all children and communities, be it boys or girls and without any discrimination as a commitment to eliminate gender disparity. Since UN's Declaration about MDGs in 2000, which talked about poverty and hunger eradication, gender equality and women empowerment, and education for all, many countries around the world have strengthened their commitment to development of human capital. However, the MDGs achievement met with a failure regards universal primary education. The 2013 data showed that 59 million children of primary-school age group were left out of school. [2] A large number of girl children—approximately 31 million—were also left out of the school. Additionally, 17 million girls were never expected to join a school. [3]

Despite the failure of MDGs, the UN as an initiator of ongoing commitment in shortening gaps in the society continuously committed itself to eliminate inequality in education for both the sexes as a move towards SDGs target.

Sustainable development goals (SDGs) were established by prioritizing zero gaps in the society. As Jawaharlal Nehru, former Indian Prime Minister revealed, "you can tell the condition of a nation by looking at the status of its women". In reality, low level of girl education is a also a contributory factor in existence of poverty. Education for women is needed to strengthen economic growth. Thus, gender equality and quality education are the highlight goals of any developmental priority.

Being one of the most populous countries in the world, Indonesia and India have similar challenges of sizable population that affects the education system. Indonesia with more than 250 million people and 17,000 islands has constraints of transportation and communication among its geographical areas, coupled with inaccessible infrastructure thereby affecting the educational facilities. [4] Besides, India with more than 1,210 million people and 35 states/union territories also faces bottlenecks in education and literacy rates. [5]

Unpredictably, the participation rate of girls in education has obviously decelerated starting from the age of 10 years. In Indonesia, in the age bracket of 10-year, girls are more likely to opt out of every 10 children who drop out—evidently 6 are girls and 4 are boys. [6] This is caused by gender disparity pertaining to cultural traditions that have militated against women and girls collectively, especially in rural areas. [7] The cultural traditions hugely influence gender segregation in the society. Men are responsible for public domain while women are responsible for domestic domain. Powerfully, the society system, economic system, and the political system are unsupportive of girl education. Therefore, the parents are sceptical about the value of education for girls. More so, with Indonesia predominantly having the largest Muslim population in the world, girls also get married at an early age. [8]

Finally, religion also plays a crucial role in discrimination against women. Lack of women in the field of education can be gauged by 14.54 percent illiteracy among girls in 2001 as compared to a 6.87 percent among boys. Likewise, in case of India, girl participation in education has been decreasing in the same age group of 10-year because of family responsibilities, such as caring of younger siblings etc. [9] However, in the early 1990s, the Indian government did provide accessible and good quality educational facilities. Apparently, the teachers were responsible for an average of 30-40 students in the class. Ultimately, the teachers discouraged girls, especially from backward/poor communities from coming to school. [10]

As it occurred in Indonesia, even Indian women's and girl's position has been inferiorly recognized, which has made value of education for girls low. [11] However, education for women and girls is a value to survive with dignity with an impact on reduction in poverty, fighting hunger, improvement in health conditions, reduction in female genital cutting and increase in self-confidence. [12] Even though the girl education has met progress in recent years, yet there is still a big gap as regards treatment of girls and boys in education impartment.

ASEAN and Girl Participation in Education

After the ASEAN Education Declaration of October 24, 2009 was established, education is a cross-cutting issue in the three pillars of sustainable economy, political security and socio-culture. ASEAN consisting of 10 member countries emphasizes education as a priority that was listed in the ASEAN Socio-Cultural Community (ASCC) blueprint. The 28 specific action lines was proposed by the ASCC blueprint for advancing and prioritizing education by 2015 to eradicate illiteracy and to ensure compulsory primary education for all and gender equality in education without discriminating on the basis of social class, geography, ethnicity, background or physical disabilities. [13]

Furthermore, working towards achieving gender equality and the empowerment of all women and girls is one of the characteristics and elements of the ASEAN community. In the overarching goals of ASEAN Community 2025, the ASCC is envisioned to move towards a more inclusive community by promoting and protecting human rights of women, children, youth, the elderly/older persons, persons with disabilities, migrant workers, ethnic minority groups, and vulnerable and marginalized groups.

In addition, the ASEAN Human Rights Declaration (AHRD) under the economic, social and cultural rights general principles has granted right to education for everyone (point no. 31). [14] Moreover, it has declared that education shall be directed for full development of human personality and sense of dignity. Primary education shall be compulsory and be made freely available to all.

The ASCC blueprint has focused on technical and vocational education and training (TVET) as an area of particular priority. Education is acknowledged as the foundation of economic integration in ASEAN countries. Likewise, AHRD declared in point number 31.2 that technical and vocational education shall be made generally available. TVET is reportedly able to develop a sense of concern about the need for opportunities and even ASEAN has acknowledged TVET as the main thrust area to generate skilful citizens.

ASEAN has actively stepped forward in dealing with economic issues also. The ASEAN community has been actively harmonizing collaboration regards university network by emphasizing on English language, youth exchange programmes, regional networks, and scholarships.

ASEAN as a regional organization has been facing hitches of girl participation in education and the implementation is still a far cry. In fact, in ASEAN countries, girl participation in education in 2010 was dismal whereas boys continued to have a greater access to primary education than girls in Cambodia, Lao PDR, Myanmar and Vietnam.

In Cambodia, the adult literacy rate was 73.9 percent in 2009 which was below the UNESCO regional average. After the Khmer Rouge regime fell over after 30 years, Cambodia faced an acute shortage of educated people. During that time, Cambodia faced a huge problem of developing an educational system until the Cambodian leaders and politicians realised that education is essential to the development of the nation. However, the education enrolment, especially of girls, received discrimination. In 2013, there were 47 percent girls participating in rural primary schools and merely 48 percent girls participating in urban primary schools. [15]

These percentages were representative of under half of the enrolments in both rural and urban areas. The children needed to walk and travel to school for almost 5 miles or more which was socially not acceptable for girls. However, similar to India's case, girls are more directed to look after their younger siblings, work alongside their parents in rice fields, and travel to urban centres to find work in factories. [16] Besides, the image of girls is also viewed inferior. The society does not see how important girls and they do not recognize them as clever as boys. [17]

In Lao PDR, the disparities strongly exists in the society among gender groups, ethnic groups, poor, non-poor, urban, rural and remote areas. This disadvantage is mostly perceived by the girls. Girls also have limited access to social services. Girls are normally assumed to stay at home to assist with the household chores. Thus, school education is not only perceived as less relevant for their future but also because parents fear for their daughters' safety far away from home, especially in the rural areas. The government has identified 47 high priority districts and 25 priority districts to improve upon infrastructural facilities for education. [18] Moreover, the society expects girls to be polite and weak, and hence girls are shy to talk or respond to the teachers. They also have fewer opportunities to participate in social activities, and resultantly, boys learn better than girls. [19]

The girls' participation rate in primary schools in 2011 was higher than the boys in the urban areas—95.4 percent of girls compared to 94.4 percent of boys. Meanwhile, in rural areas with proper road facilities, the girls' participation rate was a bit less than the boys, pegged at 84.2 percent of girls compared to 84.5 percent of boys. On the contrary, in rural areas without road infrastructure, girls' participation was significantly less compared to boys, pegged at 68.2 percent of girls in comparison to 72.3 percent boys. [20] The disparity for girls was obvious. While there were about 5 primary-school-going-aged girls in urban areas, over 30 girls in the same age group in rural areas without road were out of schools. Above all, the below poverty line population stood at 24 percent in the country.

In Myanmar, gender disparity in education has been a serious problem. Girls accounted for 49 percent of total primary enrolment, 50 percent of lower secondary enrolment, and 53 percent of upper secondary enrolment in 2011. [21] By age 15, girls were slightly more likely to be in school than boys, while the overall participation rates at this age remained low at 45.1 percent and 43.5 percent respectively. [22] The share of out-of-school children in 2009-10 dynamically altered. At primary school level, in the age bracket of 5-9 years, there were 12 percent of girls out of school compared to boys. Going forward, at middle school level in the age bracket of 10-13 years, there were 21 percent of girls out of school compared to 19 percent of boys. At the high school level, in the age group of 14-15 years, the percentage stood at 52 percent for girls opting out of school compared to boys at 47 percent. [23] Surprisingly, the Myanmar government indicated that there is no significant gender-disparity in education and the education is fully supportive of girls to get equal rights.

In contrast, obviously, bias towards girls in the society can be found regards the education system including lack of gender-sensitive curricula as well as lack of gender-sensitive classroom environment. Moreover, culturally, the society perceives the behaviour of distrust among boys, such as sexual harassment. [24] Girls are protected by parents, especially in puberty, to prevent sexual assault and harassment. The unsafe environment is the utmost reason to stop girls from pursuing education. In addition, gender-disparity, lack of facilities in the school, lack of parents' interest towards girl education and cost of education are other factors that can be attributed to wards low enrolment of girl child.

In Vietnam, the difference in gross enrolment rate in primary schools for girls and boys during the period 2012-2013 stood at 0.99 percent—110.16 percent for boys and 104.07 percent for girls. Also, in lower secondary education, there was a contrast in net enrolment rate among boys (91.17 percent) and girls (84.96 percent) in 2012-2013. [25] Likewise, in Lao PDR, the girl child participation rate was also low due to factors like gender and ethnic minority. The girls from ethnic minority were placed even worse. The Vietnamese government reported that up to 70 percent of ethnic minority girls dropped out of school in 2009. [26] The geographical area became a huge issue for girls to go to school. Distances to the school inhibited efficient school activities whereby in some cases they were even required to stay overnight and worst even was the lack of separate bathroom facilities for girls.

Indonesian Education System

Indonesian education roots from the basic fundamental jurisdiction of *Pancasila* as the state ideology and the 1945 Constitution. Article 31 of the 1945 Constitution stipulates that national education means every citizen has the right to education that is able to be responsive to the needs of the ever-changing era. The juridical law of education obviously emphasizes on education justice without segregating on the basis of religion, culture, ethnicity and language since Indonesia is multicultural country with unity in diversity. Under the Indonesian law, the national education system stipulates that a national education system should ensure equal opportunity, improvement of quality and relevance and efficiency in management to meet various challenges in the wake of changes at local, national and global level. The purpose of education is to develop Indonesian people intellectually, morally, spiritually, physically and socially. Indonesian education indicates that people are not only enhanced by their intellectual capacity, but also people are imbued with faith of God value. [27]

The education system in Indonesia is managed differently compared to other countries. There are two ministries responsible for the education system viz., the Ministry of National Education (MoNE) for general school and the Ministry of Religious Affairs (MoRA) for Islamic-based schools. MoNE is managing 84 percent schools and the remaining 16 percent are under MoRA. Although, the education system is under the responsibility of central government, yet the government extends decentralized authority to the lower administration with teacher requirement being the responsibility of district government and budget for education being the responsibility of the regional government. [28] Furthermore, Law 22/1999 stipulates about regional governance and Law 25/1999 talks about the financial balance between the central government and the regions.

The education system is organized into three levels, namely, basic education, middle or secondary education and higher education. The government insists Indonesian children from zero until 6 years to have an early childhood education. Basic education starts from age 7 and consists of six years of education in elementary school as well as three years of junior education. Middle or secondary education is comprised of three years of senior high school or senior vocational education. Higher education consists of diploma, bachelors, masters, doctoral and post-doctoral degree programmes. The education program out-of-school consists of packet A, packet B and packet C that align with the level of basic education and middle or secondary education.

Furthermore, compulsory education was established under Law number 2/1989 and Law number 20/2003. Indonesian government provides a compulsory nine-year education that covers the basic education. The Indonesian government has puts languages as a subject to the curriculum, whereby a student has to learn minimum three languages in the school, including Bahasa, a local language and a foreign language. Bahasa, as the national language, is used as a medium of language to communicate with others. Local language is kept in the curriculum to maintain the cultural aspect. A foreign language is important to align with the developments in the global context.

With a huge population, it becomes extremely difficult in providing an accessible education system in the country. The government spends only 3 percent of the GDP on education. [29] Political issues at both the government level and in the Parliament affect an effective implementation of policies and programmes thereby resulting in inadequate availability of schools. As stated by former Minister of Education Baswedan, there are 5.3 million Indonesians, with only 170,000 elementary schools, 43,000 junior high schools and just over 25,000 high schools.

These schools can serve 30,000,000 students at elementary school level and 10,000,000 students at the junior school level. The number of students is decreasing at senior high school and senior vocational school level as these schools can serve only 6,600,000 students. [30] The reason for this is that parents cannot afford the cost of education, especially in rural areas. To prove that the government fully supports the cause of education, the government eventually launched a funding program called *Bantuan Operasional Sekolah/BOS* (School Operational Assistance) program in 2005 to lessen the children participation rate at the elementary school and junior high school level. However, the school operational assistance is not sufficient enough to cover the entire operational expenses of the schools, mainly at the junior high school level.

As has been cited above, the less participation rate of Indonesian children in education is due to the economic stability of the parents. Stability of national economic growth can be addressed via the context of education. Vocational education and training is considered as a successful provision of human development that can be both competitive as well as skilful. [31] In the Indonesian society, vocational education is perceived as an alternate to academic failure. [32]

Vocational education is comprised of formal and non-formal education. It starts at vocational high school that can be continued after having pursued junior high school and then can be taken at the polytechnic level at higher education. Nevertheless, Indonesia faces an equitable vocational education across the country, especially in rural areas. In some provinces, there is only 30 percent enrolment rate at vocational high schools, whereas the target of enrolment rate must be 60 percent per province. In fact, the presence of vocational high school is a hyper reality, because vocational high schools are still male-oriented, and resultantly the girls are not able to access this mode of education.

Girl Education in Indonesia

Although the Indonesian government has paid greater attention in education over the years, in fact, the geographical and demographical circumstances still inhibit the implementation of policies successfully. Due to inadequate availability of schools, girls are forced to opt out from the school system because for many people, education is still a privilege rather than a basic human right. By the age of 10 years, girls mostly opt out of school due to family reasons. [33] This condition results in marginalization and discrimination against girls and women.

Indonesia with the highest Muslim population in the world predominantly has a social system dominated with patriarchy. Unsurprisingly, gender mainstreaming in education is inferiorly applicable. Superiority of boys and men has been explored in textbooks and curriculum systematically which enhances a negative stereotype for girls and women. Moreover, women and girls are subordinated while concluding from history, norms and social structure and there is still a long way to go to eradicate gender-bias in the society.

The girls and women are always scared through the myth of not maintaining the virginity. The girls and women are directed to avoid sexual activity before marriage *(zina)*, which is categorized as a sin.

Early marriage is a common practice in Indonesia, especially during the early days of getting periods even though they are not ready physically and mature mentally. The government established Law No. 1 in the year 1974 under the Constitution which states that girls can be married at the age of 16 years or 18 years by getting parents' permission.

However, the autonomy system offers the regional governments to establish the distinction of age-marriage-minimum. For instance, in the West-Java province, the age-marriage-minimum for girls is under 15 year old. There are 22 percent of girls marrying under the age of 15 years. [34] In Indramayu, West-Java province, a notably Islamic region, the practice of early marriage is a common matter.

As mentioned above, the indicator of marriage readiness for girls is getting the periods. The parents marry off their girls rather than letting them be single. [35] Considering the matter, West-Java province, particularly Indramayu, suffers from formidable problem of human trafficking issue in Indonesia, followed by Cirebon. [36] Approximately, 30 percent of the girls are forced into prostitution in the age group of 14-17 years. Moreover, 52.26 percent of the girls are having an early marriage.

In case of *Nusa Tenggara Timur*/East Nusa Tenggara (NTT), if the girls or women go to school out of their villages and live alone without being accompanied, the value of their dowry decreases, because they are assumed not to have virginity. Early marriage is recommended to avoid *zina,* which precisely puts girls into danger. Early marriage contributes to 50 percent of maternal mortality. Conservative parents and society, and the religion are the factors which influence the education level of girls thereby impacting their lives.

Indian Education System

India got Independence from the British colonization in 1947, two years later than Indonesia's Independence from Japanese colonization in 1945. For India and Indonesia, the colonization extremely influenced the education system. In case of India, the education was originally based on the British model, but changed over into 10 years basic education, 2 years senior secondary education and 3 years of higher education as stipulated under the National Policy on Education, 1992. [37]

The Resolution on the National Policy on Education adopted in 1968 pointed out that the great leaders of the Indian freedom movement realised the fundamental role of education and—throughout the struggle for independence—stressed the unique significance of education for national development. The Resolution further declared that the radical re-construction of education should involve the following:

1. Transformation of the system to relate it more closely to the life of the people.
2. Continuous effort to expand educational opportunity.
3. Sustained and intensive effort to raise the quality of education at all stages.
4. Emphasis on the development of science and technology.
5. Cultivation of moral and social values.

According to the Resolution, the educational system must produce young men and women of character and ability, committed to national service and development.

In a democratic set up, the role of education becomes crucial, since it can function effectively only if there is an intelligent participation of the masses in the affairs of the country.

Education, broadly perceived as a seamless continuum of life-long learning, is essential for human resource development at every age level. In a package of developmental inputs available to the community, education should form an effective means to: (a) improve the status and character of living patterns of the people, (b) help intellectual, social and emotional development of the individuals and (c) enable them to meet their basic needs of daily life, (d) satisfy cultural needs which are essential for the healthy growth of a nation and (e) stimulate the growth of the creative faculties, increase the capacity for enjoyment and develop a spirit of critical appreciation of arts, literature and other creative activities.

The long range goal of educational planning is then to make available diverse networks of facilities and programmes for education, combining formal and non-formal modes of learning. It should enable all citizens to acquire literacy, numeracy, computational skills, basic understanding of the surrounding world and functional skills of relevance to daily life and to local environment.

The intensity of the problems of education and population growth in rural areas corresponds to the educational deprivation of women. The broad priorities, therefore, should prepare the ground for the spread of literacy and primary education through socio-economic justice and to remove the traditional constraints on the status and education of rural women, in particular.

A demand for education, modernization and efficiency has to be stimulated through a general awakening and mobilisation of the rural communities especially in the educationally backward states.

The fulfilment of these objectives would lead to the development of an integrated personality in the individual, which should be the first and foremost aim of any system of education.

The Indian education system is managed by the Ministry of Human Resource Development. Currently, the MHRD works through two departments:

- Department of School Education and Literacy.
- Department of Higher Education.

Department of School Education and Literacy is responsible for development of school education and literacy in the country. It has its eyes set on the *universalisation of education* and making better citizens out of India's young brigade. For this, various new schemes and initiatives are taken up regularly and recently, those schemes and initiatives have also started paying dividends in the form of growing enrolment in schools.

Department of Higher Education takes care of what is one of the largest higher education systems of the world, just after the United States and China.

It is engaged in bringing world class opportunities of higher education and research to the country so that Indian students are not found lacking when facing an international platform. For this, the Government has launched joint ventures and signed MoUs to help the Indian students benefit from the world opinion.

The main objectives of MHRD are as under:

1. Formulating the national policy on education and to ensure that it is implemented in letter and spirit.
2. Planned development, including expanding access and improving quality of the educational institutions throughout the country, including the regions where people do not have easy access to education.
3. Paying special attention to disadvantaged groups like the poor, females and the minorities.
4. Provide financial help in the form of scholarships, loan subsidy etc. to deserving students from deprived sections of the society.
5. Encouraging international co-operation in the field of education, including working closely with the UNESCO and foreign governments as well as universities, to enhance the educational opportunities in the country.

Education and Women Empowerment in India

There is an increased awareness that education is one of the most valuable means of achieving gender equality and the empowerment of women. Education is seen as a critical factor in breaking the inter-generational cycle of transmission of poverty. The power of education lies not just in imparting formal literacy, but rather in the acquisition of skills that enable access to multiple literacy—economic, legal, health, political and media etc.

Education is a key intervention in initiating and sustaining processes of empowerment. Good quality education can help women and marginalized communities to: (a) improve their status, (b) enable them to have greater access to information and resources and (c) challenge various forms of discrimination.

Education helps strengthen democratic processes as it allows for greater and more equitable participation. Being educated leads to greater self-confidence and self-esteem. It enables engagement with development processes and institutions of governance from a position of strength. Poor women from socially disadvantaged communities are invariably not literate and therefore find themselves at a disadvantage when participating in development processes.

It is, however, important to recognise that while being literate or educated is necessary for empowerment, it does not automatically ensure it. For that a society needs an education system which is of good quality and promotes critical thinking. From the perspective of gender this means that education and literacy should enable women and girls to critically analyse their situations, raise questions about their subordination and help them make informed choices.

It is well-known that the institution of schooling is an important site for socialisation that actually reinforces rather than challenges patriarchy and gender discrimination. It is in this context that the content and pedagogy of education become critical considerations.

The focus of educational planning is generally on formal education but this is only one dimension of the educational provisioning, especially when needs of deprived women are under consideration and empowerment of women is the main objective.

Though the content of education and classroom pedagogy are critical to altering gender and other social relations it has not been paid the attention it deserves.

Efforts to make curricula gender-sensitive have been undertaken but can be considered initial attempts as they have remained largely at the level of removing stereotypes or increasing visibility and have not looked at gender in terms of social relations.

Problems related to the representation of marginalized communities continue to exist and contribute to the deep sense of alienation of these communities from the mainstream education system and a reason for children dropping out. Sexuality is addressed in a problematic manner in educational materials.

It is either related to population or reproductive health or seen as a problem associated with promiscuity and shame. Classrooms need to be transformed into spaces that can help girls think critically. Discriminatory practices based on identity-based prejudices need to be monitored and stopped. Corporal punishment, which is wide spread, needs to be checked. The role of the teacher is naturally crucial in this context.

Sexual Harassment, Violence and Women Education: Sexual harassment and violence against girls and young women within educational institutions is widespread but under-reported. While some universities have formulated guidelines and established mechanisms to deal with sexual harassment, many educational institutions still do not have policies.

Though technically the guidelines should cover schools, no efforts have been made to implement the guidelines in schools where sexual harassment is fairly common but is rarely reported. One only has the media (print and electronic) to rely on for such information.

Another area that has not received much attention is the impact of conflict and communal and sectarian violence on education. Communal and sectarian violence and long-term conflicts severely impact opportunities for girls and women's education. In volatile situations girls are kept away from schools.

In parts of India, like the North East and Kashmir, that have been experiencing conflict for several years, the ground level situation reveals that prolonged violence has negatively impacted the education systems there and the education opportunities for women and girls in various ways.

Dropout rate of girls is high because of fear, insecurity, restricted mobility, displacement, migration etc. School participation and quality of education for girls is impacted by measures to control women's sexuality and mobility, like diktats imposing a dress code by religious bodies, militants or separatist groups.

In such situations schooling and other educational interventions can bring about a semblance of normalcy and prevent alienation from the mainstream. No systematic efforts have been made to understand and monitor the impact of conflict on education, especially women and girls.

There are no policy guidelines on how to respond to the impact of violence and conflict. There are no mandated special provisions to deal with the particular problems arising out of such situations. Education provisioning, from gender perspective, should find a place in any policy on internal displacements and associated relief and rehabilitation measures.

Though the level and quality of education can be measured in a number of ways, literacy figures are essential in any measurement of educational attainment. The level of literacy is an important and the most basic index of the educational achievements of an economy.

Literacy levels in a country are a measure of its degree of commitment to social justice. A literate environment is essential for ensuring universal elementary education, reducing child mortality, curbing population growth, ensuring gender equality and acquiring essential livelihood skills.

Over the decades, literacy rates in India have shown a substantial improvement. The total literacy rate which was only 18.33 percent in 1951, rose to 52.21 percent in 1991, and further to 65.4 percent in 2001 and subsequently increased to 74.04 percent in 2011.

According to the Census of India, 2011, the literacy rate has gone up to 82.14 percent for males and 65.46 percent for females. Female literacy rate has shown much higher growth, increasing by 11.30 percentage points as against 6.29 for males thus reducing the male-female differential in literacy rates from 21.7 in 2001 to 16.68 in 2011. Literacy rates in India have risen sharply from 18.3 percent in 1951 to 74.04 percent in 2011. Nevertheless, India continues to lag behind several other developing countries in the region such as China (86 percent) and Sri Lanka (92 percent).

Conclusion

To conclude, education is the most important single factor in achieving rapid economic development and technological progress and in creating a social order founded on the values of freedom, social justice and equal opportunity. Programmes of education lie at the base of the effort to: (a) forge the bonds of common citizenship, (b) harness the energies of the people and (c) develop the natural and human resources of every part of the country.

Modernisation of syllabi, examination reforms and greater attention to issues of governance of universities and colleges, all require urgent attention. Part of the problem facing universities is the inadequate provision of budgetary resources from the governments.

Since budget resources are limited, and such resources as are available, need to be allocated to expanding primary education, it is important to recognise that the universities must make greater efforts to supplement resources from the governments.

In education, the elementary sector is besieged by numerous systemic problems such as inadequate school infrastructure, presence of single-teacher schools, high teacher absenteeism (especially in rural areas), large-scale teacher vacancies, inadequate equipment etc. This brings into focus the role of decentralization and people's participation in the provision of basic services. It is essential that control over schools and teachers should be transferred to local bodies, having a direct interest in teacher performance.

The quality of teaching in elementary schools is also not what it should be. Teacher absenteeism is widespread, teachers are not adequately trained and the quality of pedagogy is poor. These deficiencies need to be corrected to improve the quality of education at the elementary level, especially in rural areas.

One of the important links between education and development is provided by manpower development through vocationalisation of secondary education related to employment. This has to be carefully designed, based on detailed surveys of existing and potential work opportunities and of available educational and training facilities.

It should also keep in view the specific roles and responsibilities of the different agencies and ensure co-ordination at the operational level between the developmental programmes and the educational system.

Such a differentiation should normally commence after the secondary stage and may cover varying periods depending upon the vocational area, groups of occupations and the nature and level of skills needed. It envisages deepening of practical bias in the school education to be supplemented by appropriate apprenticeship in actual field, farm or factory situations.

The vocational education system suffers from deficiencies such as a low component of general education, poor linkages between the vocational education and general education streams and between the vocational education and vocational training streams. Since it creates the capability for acquiring skills, the system of general education itself, especially primary education, needs to be strengthened in the interests of skill acquisition. Education being a foundational skill, the focus on skills needs to start at the level of basic education through enlarging access and improving quality.

It also needs to be noted that the link between vocational education, vocational training and actual employment is not really known, both due to the lack of actual link and due also to the paucity of information from the labour market. This has to be addressed adequately through evolving effective systems of feedback.

Endnotes

1. Chakrabarty, K.C. (2011), "Indian Education System: Issues and Challenges", BIS Central Banker's Speeches. India.
2. UNDP (2015), "Sustainable Development Goals", available at: https://sustainabledevelopment.un.org/sdg4.
3. UNESCO (2013), "Girls' Education: The Facts", available at: http://en.unesco.org/gemreport/sites/gem-report/files/girls-factsheet-en.pdf.
4. Hendyana, S., Supriatna, A. and Imansyah, H. (2007), "Indonesia's Issues and Challenges on Quality Improvement of Mathematics and Science Education", available at: http://aadcice.hiroshima u.ac.jp/e/publications/sosho4_1-04.pdf.
5. Census of India (2011), "Size, Growth Rate and Distribution of Population", available at: http://censusindia.gov.in/2011-prov-results/data_files/india/Final_PPT_2011_chapter3.pdf.
6. UNICEF (2002), "Girl's Education in Indonesia", available at: https://www.unicef.org/indonesia/girls_education_fact_sheet_final_ENG_1_.pdf.
7. UNESCO (1998), "Girls' and Women's Education in Indonesia", available at: http://www.unescobkk.org/fileadmin/user_upload/appeal/gender/indonesia.pdf.
8. Surbakti, S. and Devasahayam T. (2015), "Women and Girls in Indonesia: Progress and Challenges", Jakarta: UNFPA.
9. Velkoff, V.A. (1998), "Women's Education in India", *Women of The World,* available at: https://www.census.gov/population/international/files/wid-

9801.pdf.

10. Ramachandran, V. (1998), "Girl's and Women Education in India", Bangkok: UNESCO.
11. DFID (2005), "Girls' Education: Towards a Better Future for All", UK: Crown Copyright.
12. Results (2009), "Why is Education for All So Important", available at: https://www.results.org/images/uploads/files/why_education_matters_11_04_09.pdf.
13. ASEAN (2016), "ASEAN Socio-Cultural Community Blueprint 2025", Jakarta: ASEAN Secretariat.
14. ASEAN (2013), "ASEAN Human Rights Declaration", Jakarta: ASEAN Secretariat.
15. Ministry of Education, Youth and Sport (MoEYS) of Cambodia (2013b), "Education Congress Report on the Education, Youth and Sport Performance in the Academic Year 2011-2012 and the Academic Year 2012- 2013 Goals", Phnom Penh: MoEYS.
16. UNESCO (2015), "Education for All 2015 National Review: Cambodia", Cambodia: EFA.
17. Velasco, E. (2001), "Why are Girls Not in School? Perceptions, Realities and Contradictions in Changing Cambodia", Bangkok: UNESCO.
18. UN (2001), "Lao People's Democratic Republic: Report on Implementation of the Brussels Programme of Action for the Least Developed Countries (2001-2010)", available at: http://www.un.org/en/conf/ldc/pdf/laos%20pdr.pdf.
19. UNESCO (2003), "Gender and Ethnicity in the Context of Equality and Access in Lao Education (Draft)", Bangkok: UNESCO.
20. UNESCO (2015), "Lao People's Democratic Republic: Education for All 2015 National Review", Bangkok: UNESCO.
21. ADB (2014), "Interim Country Partnership Strategy: Myanmar, 2012-2014", available at: https://www.adb.org/sites/default/files/linked-documents/icps-mya-2012-2014-ga.pdf.
22. UNESDOC (2015), "International Seminar on Girls' and Women's Education: Summary Report", China: UNESDOC.
23. ADB (2016), "Gender Equality and Women's Rights in Myanmar: A Situation Analysis", The Philippines: ADB.
24. Thein, P.T. (2015), "Gender Equality and Cultural Norms in

Myanmar", available at: http://www.burmalibrary.org/docs21/Society%20and%20Culture/Pansy-Tun-Thein-2015-Gender_Equality_and_Cultural_Norms_in_Myanmar-en.pdf.

25. Ministry of Education and Training (2014), "Education for All 2015 National Review: Viet Nam", Hanoi: UNESDOC.
26. Giao (2014), "Issues in Education for Vietnamese Children", available at: http://vinacapitalfoundation.org/wp-content/uploads/2014/05/VCF-Research_Issues-in- Education-for-Vietnamese-Children_20140523_V1_GV.pdf.
27. UNESCO (2013), "Girls' Education: The Facts", available at: http://en.unesco.org/gemreport/sites/gem-report/files/girls-factsheet-en.pdf.
28. UNESCO (2014), "Education System in ASEAN+6 Countries: A Comparative Analysis of Selected Educational Issues", Bangkok: UNESCO Bangkok Office.
29. UNESCO (2014), "Education System in ASEAN+6 Countries: A Comparative Analysis of Selected Educational Issues", Bangkok: UNESCO Bangkok Office.
30. Firman, H. and Tola, B. (2008), "The Future Schooling in Indonesia", *Journal of International Cooperation in Education,* Hiroshima: CICE Hiroshima University, pp. 71-84.
31. Chen, D. (2009), "Vocational Schooling, Labour Market Outcomes, and College Entry", USA: Human Development Sector Department, World Bank.
32. OECD and ADB (2015), "Education in Indonesia: Rising to the Challenges", Paris: OECD/ADB.
33. OECD (2011), "Access to Education, Participation and Progression", available at: [http://www.oecd.org/education/skills-beyond-school/48631055.pdf.
34. UNICEF (2010), "Delayed Progress: The Early Marriage Data Analysis in Indonesia", Jakarta: BPS-Statistic Indonesia.
35. Sulhan, M. (2012), "Prophetic Value of Islamic Education to Cope with Human Trafficking", *Islamic Education Journal*, 6:2, pp. 151-176.
36. Candraningrum, D., Dhewy, A. and Pratiwi, A.M. (2015), "Fear of Zina, Poor Education and Poverty: Status of Girls in Child-Marriage in Sukabumi, West-Java", *Women Journal,* 21:1, pp.

149-186.

37. Nuffic (2015), "Education System in India", Netherland: EP-NUFFIC.

5

India-ASEAN Physical Linkages

Mohd. Faheem

Abstract

This paper focuses on the opportunities and challenges of physical connectivity between India and ASEAN. Connectivity will help bring people closer, and promote trade and economic cooperation. Improving connectivity is essential for the region's prosperity, continued growth and, most importantly, poverty reduction. On the physical linkages front among India and the Association of Southeast Asian Nations (ASEAN), there are numerous projects in progressive mode to fulfil the objectivity of connectivity in the form of development of roads and railways to trap the benefits to enhance trade, investment and revival of cultural and civilizational links between India and member countries of the ASEAN. At the same time, numerous constraints are part of the process of connectivity in the form of institutional bottlenecks in India and member countries in ASEAN particularly in Myanmar and Cambodia. This chapter reveals the potential aspect of India-ASEAN connectivity and problems that exist in the process of connectivity.

Introduction

The Association of Southeast Asian Nations (ASEAN) has come a long way since its formation in Bangkok on August 8, 1967. Shifting with the paradigms of the times, it has transformed from security alliance during the Cold War into a key player of peace and prosperity in Southeast Asia. Consistent with the development of the grouping, ASEAN is also thinking beyond the ASEAN Economic Community (AEC) viewing from its relationships with dialogue partners over the years.

Historically and culturally, India has been engaging with the countries of Southeast Asia over the centuries. The names such as 'Indonesia' and 'Indochina', for instance, signify the Indian connection with Southeast Asia (Naidu, 2010: 285). However, the 'Look East Policy' gathered momentum from the early 1990s, when late P.V. Narasimha Rao, former Indian Prime Minister, delivered the 'Singapore Lecture' in 1994, addressing the significance of the relationship with countries in the Asia-Pacific region. The main reason behind this approach was that with the collapse of the former USSR, in the post-Cold War era, the 'geopolitical framework of international politics changed drastically and therefore required new measures by India to deal with the emerging reality of regional actors instead of the super powers of the Cold War period (Goswami, 2009: 4).

The essential philosophy of the 'Look East Policy' was that India finds it destiny by linking itself more and more with its Asian partners and the rest of the world and that India's future economic interests are best served by greater integration with East and Southeast Asia. The 'Look East Policy' is an attempt to forge closer and deeper economic integration with its eastern neighbours as a part of the new realpolitik in evidence in India's foreign policy, and the engagement with ASEAN is the recognition on the part of India's elite of the strategic and economic importance of the region for the country's national interests.

India became a sectoral dialogue partner of ASEAN in 1992, which was upgraded to full dialogue partnership in 1996. Since 2002, India has had annual summits with ASEAN. ASEAN-India relations were further elevated to a strategic partnership in 2012 on the occasion of the 20th anniversary of ASEAN-India relations. At the 12th ASEAN-India Summit and the 9th East Asia Summit held in Nay Pyi Taw, Myanmar, in November 2014, the 'Look East Policy' became a dynamic and action-oriented 'Act East Policy'. The 'Act East Policy' easily has been seen in Indian foreign policy in order to engage with ASEAN countries in the areas of economic, political, strategic and cultural relations.

Rationale for India-ASEAN Connectivity

The concept of ASEAN connectivity received a major institutional fillip during the 15th ASEAN Summit in Cha-am Hua Hin, Thailand on October 24, 2009. During the Summit, ASEAN Leaders held discussions on the imperative for a well-knit ASEAN with reference to its advantageous position—strategically as a strong economic regional entity, geographically bound by India in the west, China, Japan and the Republic of Korea in the Northeast, and Australia and New Zealand in the South—which reflects potential for ASEAN to lead in transforming itself into a transportation, information and communication technology (ICT) and a tourism hub of the region.

As ASEAN strives to achieve its goal of establishing a single market and become a fully integrated ASEAN community, it is clear that connectivity is a crucial factor as demonstrated by the adoption of the revised Master Plan on Connectivity (MPAC) 2025, which seeks to comprehensively connect ASEAN Member states, along with its regional and sub-regional partners, through its physical, institutional and people-to-people linkages. While MPAC is cantered on developing connectivity among ASEAN member states, it also gives due importance to connectivity with ASEAN's dialogue and strategic partners, particularly China, India, Japan, and Korea.

As per an article published in Diplomat, India is the third country after Japan and China to initiate a dedicated meeting with the ASEAN Connectivity Coordinating Committee (ACCC). It aims to support the Master Plan on ASEAN Connectivity (MPAC), and improve multimodal connectivity.

In 2010, the East Asia Summit (EAS) countries adopted a comprehensive strategy for smart, sustainable and inclusive growth [Comprehensive Asia Development Plan (CADP), 2010].

In 2010, the Master Plan on ASEAN Connectivity was adopted. It identifies key strategies and actions to enhance the region's connectivity in three dimensions: physical, institutional, and "people-to-people" (ASEAN Summit Declaration, 2010). It shows the way ahead for Asia in regional integration.

In the realm of geopolitics, ASEAN is central to economic growth and this was duly attested in New Delhi during the January 2018 India-ASEAN Summit. In that summit, there were many agreements that were made and in one of the agreements, ASEAN agreed to expand India, Myanmar and Thailand Highway express to Vietnam and India took full interest in that. From India's point of view, with expansion of this highway, there would be a positive impact on trade and at the same time it will counter China's one belt and one road project and the resultant impact on balance of power between ASEAN, China and India.

Motivations for India-ASEAN Connectivity

ASEAN and India's combined population of 1.8 billion represents one-quarter of the world's population. The combined gross domestic product (GDP) exceeds US$ 4.5 trillion. By 2025, India's consumer market is expected to become the fifth largest in the world, while in Southeast Asia, middle-class households will double to 163 million. Both regions are also experiencing a demographic dividend—60 percent of ASEAN's population is below 35 years old, while India is projected to be the world's youngest country with an average age of 29 by 2020 (Lee Hsien Loong, Prime Minister of Singapore, The Straits Times, 2018). It was noted over time that major powers of Asia have evolved consensus in allowing ASEAN to take driver's seat with reference to the efforts towards resurgence of the Asian people.

Hence, the 'ASEAN Way' has come to be a prominent and strong proposition regards the search for pan-Asian identities and values. With the constantly evolving regional architecture entailing rising competition in global trade, changing political equations, the task of maintaining ASEAN's centrality is a challenging task. Connectivity with nations beyond the region is an equally important driving force of ASEAN connectivity.

The issues related to geopolitical uncertainty is also key to India-ASEAN connectivity. From securing sea routes to trade routes and lines of communications, there are several strategic complexities on which both India and ASEAN can cooperate.

Flow of Trade between ASEAN and India

India has been an important partner of ASEAN since 1992. At present, besides ASEAN-India Free Trade Agreement (FTA) which is in effect since January 2010 at the regional level, Bay of Bengal Initiative for Multi-Sectoral and Technical Cooperation (BIMSTEC) and Mekong-Ganga Cooperation at sub-regional and Comprehensive Economic Partnership Agreements (CEPAs) with Singapore, Malaysia, Indonesia and Thailand at bilateral level are in effect.

As per MEA, Government of India, the India-ASEAN trade and investment relations have been growing steadily, with ASEAN being India's fourth largest trading partner. India's trade with ASEAN has increased to US$ 70 billion in 2016-17 from US$ 65 billion in 2015-16. India's export to ASEAN has increased to US$ 30 billion in 2016-17 from US$ 25 billion in 2015-16. According to a study by the Economic Research Institute for ASEAN and East Asia (ERIA), an enhanced ASEAN-India connectivity could result in cumulative gains of over five percent of gross domestic product (GDP) for Cambodia, Myanmar, Thailand, and Viet Nam, and gains of over two percent of GDP for India.

Indian businesses must recognize the opportunities presented by ASEAN's growth and economic integration. It will be important for Indian businesses to understand their strength in the ASEAN market and to tailor their strategies accordingly. The importance of India's current relationship with ASEAN and its future potential for mutually beneficial growth will require greater political, economic, and diplomatic engagement with ASEAN. ASEAN's geo-strategic importance stems from many factors, including the strategic location of member countries and the large shares of global trade that pass through regional waters.

Physical Connectivity between ASEAN-India

Connectivity between ASEAN and India comes with the blueprint of ASEAN-India Connectivity which was prepared in 2010 when India gave a push to its 'Look East Policy' under the United Progressive Alliance government. It was then continued by the present National Democratic Alliance government under the revamped 'Act East Policy'.

A number of initiatives have been taken by ASEAN and India towards better connectivity, consistent with the Master Plan on Connectivity (MPAC) which clearly defines specific initiatives and sets clear targets. The MPAC contains 19 strategies and 84 key actions under three dimensions—physical, institutional and people-to-people. Under physical connectivity, 7 strategies and 32 key actions were drawn up with the view to expanding and improving road, rail, inland waterways, maritime and air linkages. At present, there are many modes of connectivity that bind ASEAN and India. Foremost among these are national and regional connectivity projects being developed to facilitate and enhance trade and investment and boost the untapped economic potential of both the regions. There is a proposal to build the 'Asian Highway' and 'Asian Railway Link'.

The proposed geographical niche for the Asian Highway is the Imphal (India)-Tamu (Myanmar) road going on to Kalemyo railway onto Mandalay in Myanmar. Four lane Asian Highway is also sought between New Delhi-Singapore linked to Kuala Lumpur, Ho Chi Minh City, Phnom Penh, Bangkok, Vientiane, Yangon, Mandalay, Kalemyo, Tamu, Dhaka, and Kolkata. Road construction has already started from Tamu to Kalemyo, Myanmar (Goswami, 2009). Apart from this regional connectivity, the three most significant regional connectivity projects between ASEAN and India are the India-Myanmar-

Thailand Trilateral Highway, the Kaladan Multimodal Transit Transport Project (KMTTP), and the Mekong-India Economic Corridor (MIEC).

India-Myanmar-Thailand Trilateral Highway (IMTTH)

The first move towards the establishment of India-Myanmar-Thailand Trilateral Highway (IMTTH) was conceived at an IMT Trilateral Ministerial meeting in Yangon in 2002. The India-Myanmar-Thailand Trilateral Highway is a cross-border road network of 1,360 km. from Moreh-Tamu on the India-Myanmar border to Mae Sot on the Myanmar-Thailand border. The project is funded by the governments of three countries, Asian Development Bank and the World Bank.

The IMTTH is divided into three phases with phase I taken up in 2005 and covering construction of 78 km. of new roads, upgradation of about 400 km. of roads, construction of all-weather approach lanes, and rehabilitating and reconstructing of weak or distresses bridges. As agreed during the joint Task Force Meeting on IMTTH, held on September 10-11, 2012 in New Delhi, India is constructing the Kalewa to Yargi portion (132 km.) of the IMTTH, Myanmar would construct the Yargi-Monywa portion, and Thailand is developing the Hpa-An-Mae Sot (Thailand) portion.

The importance of the IMT highway is a permanent asset for the three countries and there is on a sub-regional level, the possibilities of creating a development corridor with rural development projects, special economic zones and exclusive economic zones which would be a boon for the people of the region. The project's importance can hardly be overstated. Once completed, it would greatly enhance the connectivity between the Mekong sub-region and India. It would also be a game changer for the Indian North-East, which shares 96 percent of its border with other countries and only four percent with the rest of India.

Kaladan Multimodal Transit Transport Project (KMTTP)

The Kaladan Multimodal Transit Transport Project (KMTTP) connecting Indian ports on the eastern side and Sittwe port in Mtanmar through a riverine transport corridor and road in Mizoram is considered to provide an alternate trade route to the North-East (Sharma, 2008). In April 2008, the Indian government signed an agreement with the Burmese military junta for the Kaladan Multi-Modal Transit Transport Project. The project connects the landlocked area of North-East India with the sea via Western Burma (Myanmar) and open up trade routes to Southeast Asia (Srinivasan, V., 2008).

The KMTTP will reduce distance from Kolkata to Sittwe by approximately 1328 km. and would also reduce the need to transport goods through the narrow Siliguri corridor in India, also known as Chicken's Neck. This project includes a waterway component of 158 km. on Kaladan River from Sittwe to Paletwa in Myanmar and a road component of 109 km. from Paletwa to Zorinpui along the India-Myanmar border in Mizoram. Through this project, the connectivity between India's North-East and Myanmar will improve which would enhance several economic activities between the two countries.

As a matter of fact, due to very weak connectivity between Myanmar and North-East India and mainland India, the vision of well-connected ASEAN-India remains blurred. Because of the geographical setting and prevalence of conflict-ridden atmosphere, especially separatist tendencies along the borders, the progress of connectivity initiatives has been very slow. This project will surely boost connectivity between India's North-Eastern part and Myanmar.

Similarly, North-East India has remained underdeveloped and politically unstable on account of very poor connectivity with mainland India. However, the Government of India has taken up a number of initiatives to bridge this development gap by encouraging investment in the social sector. The Kaladan Multimodal Transit Transport Project is one of such initiatives basically designed to open an alternate access route connecting North-East India and mainland India through Chin and Rakhin in Myanmar (Kimura F., Kudo T. and Umezaki So, 2011).

Mekong-India Economic Corridor (MIEC)

The Mekong-India Economic Corridor (MIEC) connects South and Southeast Asia. It shall integrate the Mekong countries viz. Vietnam, Myanmar, Thailand, and Cambodia with India. It will help reduce the transit distance between India and ASEAN countries. MIEC is an extended version of Southern Economic Corridor (SEC). MIEC runs through development stages and passes through ASEAN member countries such as Cambodia, Kanchanaburi in Thailand and Dawei in Myanmar. The MIEC includes development of Dawei Deep Sea Port (2020) and building of a highway between Kanchanaburi and Dawei (by 2020) among others.

In order to establish a linkage between Bangkok and Chennai, an access route from Bangkok to the Andaman Sea is proposed to be opened by constructing a highway connecting Kanchanaburi (Thailand) and Dawei (Myanmar). The comprehensive Dawei projects include a deep sea port, special economic zones, power plants and so forth. It was noted that a deep sea port would open up opportunities for firms operating in Bangkok in particular and the region in general along the MIEC by opening up of a new shipping route to India and on the other hand firms in Chennai in particular and India in general are expected to have a relatively inexpensive and alternate access to ASEAN countries.

Opportunities and Constraints

The connectivity plays a positive role in order to enhance relations between India and ASEAN. It is well known that India wants to evolve a regional architecture based on the twin principles of shared security and shared prosperity. India is looking for a deeper economic and strategic engagement with the ASEAN region by maintaining improved connectivity.

From India's point of view, time is for enhancing maritime security, trade and investment, education and cultural heritage among the member countries of ASEAN. These are important markers of 'Look Act Policy' in order to engage with Southeast Asia and in enhancing strategic ties with ASEAN across the 3Cs. These 3Cs are commerce, connectivity and culture.

It is imperative to talk about the opportunities inherent in physical connectivity and they seemed to be many: firstly, North-East India would be the gateway to Southeast Asia. As former Indian External Affairs Minister in 2007 opined, "we are involved in a variety of cross-border development projects with Myanmar in diverse fields such as roads, railways, telecommunications, information technology, science and technology, power, etc.". These development projects improving connectivity between North-East and western Myanmar in particular and between India and ASEAN in general and are expected to give an impetus to bilateral trade between India and ASEAN. Through connectivity, it is expected that development deficit in North-East part of India can be overcome by integrating it and the Southeast Asian region ushering in prosperity for the entire region.

Secondly, India has played an advantageous role of cultural and civilization links with the region of Southeast Asia. Historically, the culture of India has impacted societies of Southeast Asia in the form of art, music, language, and mythology. Enhancing the existing connectivity between the two multi-cultural societies would revive the free movement of people which has happened in the yesteryears. This approach of soft power provides ample opportunity to India in general and North-East region in particular to connect economically through connectivity with the region of Southeast Asia.

Thirdly, connectivity would gradually change the geopolitical landscape of the region. India is relatively politically engaged and well placed. As compared to great powers which have had a history of interference and intervention, India has always been a benign power and the spread of its influence has always been peaceful. Also, the connectivity has enabled India to build strong security links with the countries of Southeast Asia.

Fourthly, the possibility of larger economic integration through connectivity among South Asia, Southeast Asia and North-East part of India would extend economic and political gains resulting in these countries becoming powerhouses of the region.

Connectivity is not only about building physical infrastructure but also about encouraging investment flows. Although different advantages through connectivity exist, yet at the same time, there are various constraints that have surfaced. The North-Eastern states have extremely limited connectivity within their own borders making any effort to connect the region to other parts of India and Myanmar economically unviable. Secondly, the Myanmar factor is crucial because of the locational leverage of Myanmar which will emerge as a crucial factor in connecting Southeast Asia to India for it is the only land bridge available. Myanmar offers a very conducive geographical setting to ASEAN countries spreading across southward and eastward of it. On the other hand, North-Eastern region of India connects mainland India with Myanmar. Out of eight North-Eastern states four states, namely Arunachal Pradesh, Manipur, Mizoram and Nagaland share border with Myanmar.

Conclusion

Physical linkages bring a positive change for the people of different regions in term of prosperity. In this regard, the ten nations of Southeast Asia and India have been working on connectivity through different projects to provide economic integration between India and the member countries. There are numerous initiatives taken by ASEAN and India in order to enhance connectivity. In the major initiative there is the Master Plan on Connectivity (MPAC) which works under the three dimensions—physical, institutional and people-to-people. Under physical connectivity, various projects are running in order to expand and improve road, rail, inland waterways, maritime and air linkages. At present, there are many modes of connectivity that bind ASEAN and India. Foremost among there are national and regional connectivity projects such as the India-Myanmar-Thailand Trilateral Highway, the Kaladan Multimodal Transit Transport Project (KMTTP), and the Mekong-India Economic Corridor (MIEC).

These projects are being developed to facilitate and enhance trade and investment and boost the untapped economic potential of both the regions. At the same time, these projects also have obstacles to complete. The foremost advantages through connectivity from India's point of view keeping in view the dynamics of a single market is geo-strategic, trade, and investment and that it would further enhance the development of North-Eastern part of India. There are also great benefits through connectivity including revival of cultural and civilization links between the two multicultural societies. Connectivity plays an important role for India in the form of political engagement in a well placed manner and would help in building a strong security link with the member countries of ASEAN.

In a larger point of view, connectivity plays a very important role to bring three different regions of South Asia, Southeast Asia and North-Eastern part of India in the form of a single entity based on economic integration. There are various constraints that have surfaced mainly lack of infrastructure in North-East region of India and the underdevelopment of Myanmar which is very crucial to connect Southeast Asia with India. There are also bottlenecks related to supply-side constraints which need to be overcome.

References

De, P. (2011), "ASEAN-India Connectivity: An Indian Perspective", in Kimura, F. and S. Umezaki (eds.), 'ASEAN-India Connectivity: The Comprehensive Asia Development Plan', Phase II, ERIA Research Project Report, 2010, Jakarta: ERIA, pp. 95-150.

Goswami, N. (2009), "Looking East through India's Northeast: Identifying Policy Challenges and Outlining the Responses", IDSA Occasional Paper No.2, Institute for Defence Studies and Analyses: New Delhi.

Kimura, F., T. Kudo and S. Umezaki (2011), "ASEAN-India Connectivity: A Regional Framework and Key Infrastructure Projects", in Kimura, F. and S. Umezaki (eds.), 'ASEAN-India Connectivity: The Comprehensive Asia Development Plan', Phase II, ERIA Research Project Report 2010, Jakarta: ERIA, pp. 1-56.

Plummer, Michael G., Peter J. Morgan and Ganeshan Wignaraja (2016), (eds.), "Connecting Asia: Infrastructure for Integrating South and Southeast Asia", Edward Elgar Publishing Limited, United Kingdom.

Sharma, Ashok B. (2008), "India, Myanmar Expect Kaladan Project to Increase Border Trade", *The Financial Express*, New Delhi, April 4, available at:
http://www.financialexpress.com/news/India-Myanmar-expects-Kaladan-project-to-increase-bordertrade/292285.

Srinivasan, V. (2008), "Indian, Myanmar Sign Pact on Kaladan Project", *The Hindu Business Line*, April 3, available at:
http://www.thehindubusinessline.com/2008/04/03/stories/2008040350591200.htm.

6

A Perspective on India-ASEAN Economic Engagements

A.N. Sarkar

Abstract

Founded in 1967, the Association of Southeast Asian Nations (ASEAN) has emerged as one of the fastest growing regions of the world. ASEAN covers the Southeast Asian region. The ASEAN Member nations have a vast potential for pro-active and participatory engagement as well as regional economic cooperation, given the opportunities; bulk of which are as yet unexplored. The paper, among other things, covers the macroeconomic settings of the ASEAN countries, Indo-ASEAN economic relations and discusses future prospects.

Introduction

The Southeast Asian region has emerged as one of the fastest growing regions in the world, on the back of its strong agriculture, manufacturing and services sector. The existing ecosystem in the region supports sourcing, manufacturing and shipping of finished goods from these markets. The Association of Southeast Asian Nations (ASEAN) was established on August 8, 1967 in Bangkok, Thailand, with the signing of the ASEAN Declaration (Bangkok Declaration) by its founding members (Figure 6.1). [1]

As per ASEAN, the name 'ASEAN' is protected under Article 6 of the 'Paris Convention' for the Protection of Industrial Property adopted in 1883 and revised in Stockholm in 1967. The ASEAN Free-Trade Area (AFTA), which was established on January 28, 1992, includes a Common Effective

Preferential Tariff (CEPT) to promote the free flow of goods and services between member states. Within this region, the CLMV (Cambodia, Lao PDR, Myanmar, and Vietnam) countries have begun attracting greater attention of the global economic community, given their huge economic potential for future development. [2]

Figure 6.1: ASEAN Members

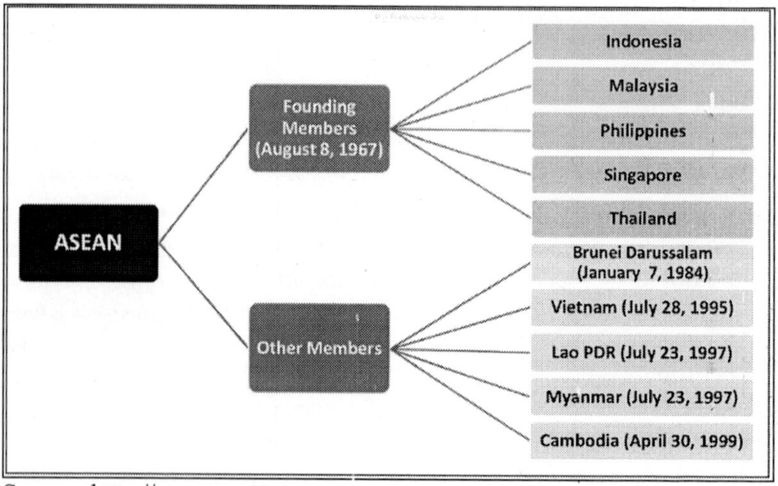

Source: http://www.asean.org

India-ASEAN Economic Cooperation

India and ASEAN have been engaging through the vision laid out by the 'Look East Policy' and the 'Act East Policy', and also through the frameworks of India-ASEAN FTA in Goods (2009) and India-ASEAN FTA in Services (2014). In fact, India and ASEAN are mutually indispensable for each other in terms of resources, sea routes, security, potential markets, investments, and value chains, and most of them are connected through the Indian Ocean as well. As per the website of the Ministry of External Affairs, 2016, "India's focus on a strengthened and multi-faceted relationship with

ASEAN is an outcome of the significant changes in the world's political and economic scenario since the early 1990s and India's own march towards economic liberalisation.

India's search for economic space resulted in the 'Look East Policy'. The 'Look East Policy' has today matured into a dynamic and action-oriented 'Act East Policy'. The Prime Minister, at the 12th ASEAN India Summit, and the 9th East-Asia Summit held in Nay Pyi Taw, Myanmar, in November 2014, formally enunciated the Act East Policy".

Also, the Ministry of External Affairs, Government of India (2016) further adds that "Apart from ASEAN, India has taken other policy initiatives in the region that involve some members of ASEAN like BIMSTEC, MGC etc. India is also an active participant in several regional forums like the Asia-Europe Meeting, East-Asia Summit, ASEAN Regional Forum, ASEAN Defence Ministers' Meeting + (ADMM+) and Expanded ASEAN Maritime Forum. There has been a steady progress in the ASEAN-India partnership since the 'Look East Policy' was launched in 1991. India became sectoral dialogue partner in 1992 and full dialogue partner in 1996". [3] Since 2002, India has annual Summits with ASEAN along with China, Japan and Republic of Korea. [4]

Since the early 1990s, the economic relationship between India and ASEAN has improved significantly. In 1992, India was admitted as a sectoral dialogue member of ASEAN and was granted the status of a full dialogue partner by December 1995. [5] The ties between the two entities have progressed substantively through cooperation in various fields.

The 'Look East Policy' adopted by India in the 1990s, along with its liberalisation programme and economic reforms, has become important not only with regard to trade flows in goods but also in the trade of services. At the beginning of 2010, the AIFTA came into effect, promising greater bilateral trade. The FTA only covered the trade in goods between the two parties with the prospect of liberalising regulations on more than 90 percent of traded goods (ASEAN: www.aseansec.org). It is noteworthy, that the FTA will eventually include products such as crude and refined palm oil, coffee, tea, and black pepper, all of which are protected in their domestic markets.

Studies by Sundararaman (2009) and Batra (2009) have focused on various aspects of the trade agreement. India now stands as ASEAN's fourth biggest trading partner and accounts for ten percent of India's global trade. Also, Asher et al. (2001) and Sosaestro (2003) argued that India has been a reliable partner and has contributed to political and economic stability in the region. ASEAN has made significant contribution to peace, stability and economic progress in the region. India has civilizational relations with the ASEAN member countries. India became a sectoral dialogue partner at ASEAN 1992 and initiated India's 'Look East Policy'. They entered into a strategic partnership in 2004 and adopted an action plan (Yong, 2005).

Services Sector Prospects

India and ASEAN entered into the ASEAN-India FTA in Services in 2014. Out of the ASEAN economies, Singapore, the Philippines, Malaysia, and Thailand have developed the strongest services sector as a result of economic liberalization and deregulation. Singapore has experienced the greatest success, thanks to a transparent legal framework (including strict intellectual property laws), political stability, and a liberalized economy that makes the country a favoured destination for foreign investment and specialized services. It operates the world's fourth-biggest foreign exchange market and invests heavily in ASEAN. Malaysia now has the region's largest bond market and has had some of the world's largest initial public offerings in 2012, and has established an extensive Islamic-banking sector. In total, financial services make up 12 percent of the country's GDP. [6]

Some ASEAN economies have already seen substantial developments in higher-end services industries. Singapore and Malaysia are already important players in finance, banking, and trade. Along with Thailand, these countries are also heavily investing in private healthcare services to meet growing regional demand. Exports of information-technology products reached US$ 258 billion in 2010, just over a quarter of the revenue from all ASEAN exports. [7]

ICT services industries, which employ more than 11 million people and generate US$ 32 billion across the region, have also been expanding. In 2011, ASEAN released the Information and Communications Technology Master Plan, 2015, a framework to collaborate on expanding the reach of services, such as broadband and telecommunications infrastructure, further develop innovation capacities, and enhance region's attractiveness to foreign investors. [8] The information technology and business process outsourcing (IT/BPO) industries in the Philippines grew 24 percent from 2010 to 2011 and produced US$ 11 billion in revenues. [9] The world's largest location for call centres is no longer India but the Philippines, a country that aims to grow its outsourcing in other fields, notably healthcare, finance, human resources, and computer-game development. [10]

The services sector along with the industry accounted for more than 80 percent of the GDP of most ASEAN economies. The share of services sector has continued to increase considerably in the region. [11] The signing of the ASEAN-India FTA in Services in 2014 has created opportunities for both India and ASEAN to engage in various services sector areas.

Hong Kong and Singapore are among the top 10 export destinations for India, while only Singapore ranks among the top ten as an importer. India accounts for barely three percent of ASEAN's share of international trade (Batra, 2009). In 2009, ASEAN accounted for nine percent of India's total imports and 11 percent of total exports (Malkani and Shah, 2010). However, it can be expected that growth in demand for ASEAN goods is likely to rise given India's increasing domestic demand, favourable demographics and rising domestic investments.

Among the WTO members, India is eleventh with regard to its share in world commercial services and ranks among the top export countries in financial services, telecommunications and information services, and construction, as well as the cultural, personal and recreational services. In addition, export of commercial services in Asia has seen double-digit growth rates in the areas of commercial transportation and travel over the past few years. [12]

India's age structure favours development for variable fields in the services sector. In contrast to other major Asian nations, India's working population will increase rather than decrease for another 30 years. Within ASEAN, only Cambodia and Laos have an increasing working population while the share of people aged 15 to 64 will decrease in all other ASEAN nations by 2020. [13] This trend will lead to increasing demand of services in ASEAN and India will prove to be a good partner to reduce and maybe even overcome this shortage. Additionally, ASEAN nations will face shortage of skilled labour, a factor that could be substituted by India. Due to their enormous growth in the past years, economies like Malaysia, Singapore and Thailand face shortages in manpower at all skill levels (Mukul et al., 2001).

FDI and AEC

In 1992, ASEAN forged a deeper economic understanding in the region through the conclusion of an agreement to set up the ASEAN Free-Trade Area (AFTA). This agreement was aimed to attract more intra-ASEAN foreign direct investment (FDI) through active liberalisation of restrictions within the ASEAN countries. In 1998, the ASEAN Investment Area was formed and is now considered to be the most significant attempt by ASEAN at liberalising FDI restrictions in the region (Plummer, 2009). To create stronger regional economic integration, ASEAN decided to create a single market through ASEAN Economic Community (AEC). [14] Through the formation of the AEC, ASEAN aimed to achieve a single market and production base in a highly competitive economic region with equitable economic development and one which is fully integrated into the global economy (ASEAN, 2010). ASEAN's continued emphasis on liberalising FDI restrictions in the last two decades thus emphasises the importance of FDI in the economic progress of the region.

The ASEAN Free Trade Area aims to increase ASEAN's competitive edge as a production base geared for the world market through trade and investment liberalisation and closer economic cooperation. Currently, four main ASEAN agreements seek to achieve this objective. These are as under: [15]

- Agreement on the Common Effective Preferential Tariff Scheme for the ASEAN Free-Trade Area (CEPT-AFTA), which was signed in 1992;
- ASEAN Framework Agreement on Services (AFAS), which was signed in 1995;
- Basic Agreement on the ASEAN Industrial Cooperation Scheme (AICO), which was signed in 1996; and
- Framework Agreement on the ASEAN Investment Area (AIA), which was signed in 1998. A close look at the main features of these agreements and their implementation deserves an overview of AFTA.

Conclusion

Under the new framework of 'Act East Policy', one would naturally expect a more integrated India-ASEAN relationship, especially in the services sector. ASEAN promotes close coordination between government and the private sector. Communication with national governments in ASEAN should be kept open so that government is aware of private sector concerns and is able to understand them. In this way, these concerns are clearly and aptly conveyed in the various ASEAN integration fora so that a balance of benefits in ASEAN economic integration and in the FTAs is achieved.

Endnotes

1. ASEAN members include Indonesia, Malaysia, Philippines, Singapore and Thailand. Later, Brunei Darussalam joined on January 7, 1984, Vietnam on July 28, 1995, Lao People's

Democratic Republic (Lao PDR) and Myanmar on July 23, 1997, and Cambodia on April 30, 1999, making up its ten Member States of ASEAN.

2. Website of ASEAN.
3. Website of Ministry of External Affairs, Government of India.
4. There are 30 Dialogue Mechanisms cutting across all the sectors including 7 ministerial level meetings.
5. Then it became a member of the Asian Regional Forum (ARF). Subsequently, India was invited to be a member of the East Asian Summit in 2005.
6. Report: Investing in ASEAN, 2011-2012.
7. "Regulatory Reforms Needed Towards 2015 ASEAN Economic Bloc", *GMA News*, July 23, 2012.
8. ASEAN ICT Master Plan, 2015.
9. Philippines IT-BPO industry hits 2011 growth targets, 2012.
10. http://www.dost.gov.ph/index.php?option=com_content&view=article&id=1096:after-dominating-call-centers-philippine-it-bpo-seeks-world-leadership-in-four-more-fast-growing-services&catid=1:latest&Itemid=150.
11. In 2012, services sector accounted for the highest share of GDP in eight ASEAN Member States.
12. "International Trade Statistics 2010", World Trade Organization, available at:
www.wto.org/english/res_e/statis_e/ its2010_e/its10_toc_e.htm.
13. United Nations, Population Division, http://esa.un.org.
14. ASEAN aims to build on past agreements, such as the AFTA and ASEAN Investment Area, and work towards achieving a free and open investment regime in the AEC to further attract both intra- and extra-ASEAN FDI.
15. https://asean.org/asean-economic-community.

References

ASEAN (2010), "ASEAN Strategic Action Plan for SME Development 2010-015", Jakarta: ASEAN, 2010, 3.

ASEAN (2013), "ASEAN Economic Community Blueprint", 6th print, ASEAN Secretariat, Jakarta, Indonesia, available at: http://www.aseansec.org/5187-10.pdf.

Asher, Mukul G., Rahul Sen and Sadhana Srivastava (2001), "ASEAN-India: Emerging Economic Opportunities", Centre for Freedom and Development Studies, May, available at:

www.cpdsindia.org/emergingeconomic.htm.

Batra, A. (2009), "India-ASEAN FTA: A Critique", *IPCS*, Issue Brief No. 116, September.

ERIA (2011), "The Jakarta Framework: Moving AEC Forward into 2015 and Beyond", Jakarta: ERIA.

Malkani, Rohini and Anushka Shah (2010), "India Macroscope: India's Growing Labour Force—Boon or Bane?", Monthly Monitor, Citigroup Global Markets, July 23.

Sosaestro, H. (2003), "ASEAN: Regional Economic Cooperation and its Institutionalization", Working Paper No. 71, Centre for Strategic and International Studies, Jakarta.

Sundararaman, Shankari (2010), "India-ASEAN FTA: To be or Not to be", *Deccan Chronicle,* April 14, available at: www.deccanchronicle.com.

UNCTAD (various years), "UNCTAD Handbook of Statistics", United Nations Conference on Trade and Development, Geneva, Switzerland.

Yong, Ong Kenk (2005), "Advancing the ASEAN-India Partnership in the New Millennium", Discussion Paper No. 96, Research and Information System for the Non-Aligned and Other Developing Countries, New Delhi.

7

India-ASEAN Transport Connectivity

M. Absar Alam and Sarfaraaj Nasir

Introduction

India's quest of attaining seamless physical connectivity with Southeast Asia is moving on in the right direction but faces certain bottlenecks as well. With the objective to strengthen India's outreach in Southeast Asian region, 'Look East Policy' was initiated by the Narasimha Rao government and rigorously persuaded by several governments thereafter particularly by the Vajpayee government. The successive governments focused on India's strong cultural and civilisational linkages with Southeast Asian countries. This is in fact, the reason that India's 'Look East Policy' had deep cultural and civilizational roots, particularly religious (Osius and Mohan, 2013). [1] Even, Indian Diasporas are ubiquitous in Southeast countries and make strong presence in both business and politics. The 'Look East Policy' transformed to 'Act East Policy' recently, which is said to be a more pro-active approach towards India-ASEAN relations.

It is believed that exploitation of potential trade between India and Southeast Asia is much affected by the transport connectivity between India and other Southeast Asian countries. Therefore, India's policy to cooperate with Southeast Asia has multiple facets. It deals with Southeast Asian countries at regional, sub-regional and bilateral level. At regional level, India has been negotiating with Association of Southeast Asian Nations (ASEAN) in various areas such as trade in goods and services, investment, transport connectivity and strategic relations, among others.

There are many aspects to discuss when it comes to India-ASEAN partnership particularly aspects which directly impact geopolitical situation in Asia and the Pacific. Moreover, with the growing economic footprints of both ASEAN and India at the global level, India's partnership with ASEAN in the areas of trade and investment has gained academic importance.

However, while examining India's relations with ASEAN, the present paper discusses developments in establishing physical connectivity between India and ASEAN. There are several modes of transport connectivity including rail, road, sea and air. But this chapter examines the recent developments in rail and road transport, while taking into account the importance of other modes of connectivity.

Transport Connectivity High on Agenda

Strengthening transport connectivity between India and ASEAN has its own importance. India is now the fastest growing economy in the world and ASEAN also has member countries with high level of economic growth. The countries of the region are gradually scaling up to become centres of major economic activities in the world. In addition, majority of countries in ASEAN are developing countries with similar traits that India possesses.

Therefore, India's physical integration with ASEAN has not only bilateral consequences but also potential consequences for facilitating South-South Cooperation between the two most populated regions of Asia and also the world, i.e. South Asia and Southeast Asia. This translates into high economic significance of strengthening transport connectivity between India and Southeast Asia.

Connectivity not only facilitates trade between countries but also enables countries to increase their economic potential and further leads to the strengthening of cultural and other ties (De, 2005). [2] Interestingly, India and countries of ASEAN region have been thriving through the centuries owing to their cultural and religious ties. One of the important examples of this is strong following of Buddhism which originated in India and Islam which has the second largest followers in India.

India's geo-economic and geopolitical interests are other important reasons for improving India's physical connectivity with ASEAN. Countries in South Asia and Southeast Asia have a legacy of colonial past and therefore, they have legacy of issues which directly and indirectly deal with political and strategic interests of the countries. In the past, a majority of countries in ASEAN had common ground of struggling against the colonial masters. During the post-colonial period, these countries are hesitantly open to other partners in the world. Such apprehensions are also visible today. Therefore, they are watching Chinese strategic interests closely, despite the fact that their economic interdependence is very high with China. India has the same legacy and has many geopolitical conflicts with China. It is in this context, that India's improved position and its strategic as well as economic footprints in ASEAN region is viewed as a potential challenge to existing Chinese footprints (Hong, 2007). [3]

A diversion of political interests between India and ASEAN countries was eminent during the yearly years of second half of the 20th century owing to strong conflict between communist and capitalist ideas. Such building blocks have also been rooted in India. During the Cold War period, India's positioning at global forums had some ideological breakaway from ASEAN as a group. This breakaway of paths is destined to converge but at a slower pace. After a long period of ideological differences, first meeting between India and ASEAN was held in 1980 almost 17 years after the establishment of ASEAN. However, India's relations with ASEAN remained unchanged and the progress was insignificant. Visits by Indian Prime Ministers like Indira Gandhi and Rajiv Gandhi in ASEAN region outlined a roadmap to start negotiations with the region's group. Yet, the formal partnership needed much more efforts.

Gradual movement of ASEAN countries towards democracy further cemented efforts made by India. Interestingly, India launched its 'Look East Policy' in 1992, a concrete effort outlining India's approach in strengthening its political, economic and strategic relations with ASEAN. India's foreign policy focuses on ASEAN through both bilateral as well as regional institutions (Sikri, 2009). [4] This was succeeded by the new 'Act East Policy'.

Considering the multi-pronged importance of India's physical integration with ASEAN, development of transport infrastructure is high on agenda under the ambit of India-ASEAN cooperation. India and other countries of ASEAN are working both at bilateral and regional levels to realize the goals of seamless transport connectivity. In the next sections, the paper discusses development plans having potential to strengthen India-ASEAN connectivity.

India's Connectivity Plans with ASEAN

Transport connectivity through rail and road is India's key endeavour in establishing its relations with ASEAN countries. This is viewed as one of the alternate connectivity routes when compared with traditional sea routes. In this regard, a notable idea was proposed in 2003 for establishing road and rail linkages by the then Prime Minister of India, Atal Bihar Vajpayee (MEA, 2003). [5] Idea of seamless rail linkages from New Delhi (India) to Hanoi (Vietnam) was a key which is yet to be connected due to missing links between countries particularly between India and Myanmar.

For direct connectivity between India and Hanoi through railways there are missing links in Myanmar from Tamu to Kaley around 128 kms. (Htun et al., 2011) [6], and from Diphu to Moreh in India (De, 2011). [7] Establishment of rail linkages between India and ASEAN countries are further compared with the objectives to establish road linkages from India to Southeast Asia. The idea was vigorously advocated at several national and international forums including United Nation's Economic and Social Commission for Asia and the Pacific (ESCAP). An intergovernmental agreement came into force in 2005 aimed at development of highway network connecting countries of the Asia and the Pacific (ESCAP, 2016). [8]

However, establishing non-sea connectivity from India in particularly and South Asia in general to Southeast Asia has several constraints embracing geographical, physical and political. One of the major geographical constraints is that the rivers are flowing from Himalayas to the Indian Ocean. The North-South routes of river cutting across mainland in South and Southeast Asia traditionally imposed for adopting routes through sea. It may be noted that establishing road and rail passing through rivers require heavy investments in the construction of bridges over the rivers. Such investment makes development of land transport costly particularly when the low cost sea routes are available. The geographical feature of the land mass in South and Southeast Asia include not only rivers flowing from North towards South but also presence of mountainous terrain like Naga Hills in India, and Chin Hills and Shan Hills in Myanmar. These features cause natural bottlenecks in the development of land transport. In fact, mountainous terrain along Indo-Myanmar border blocked the natural trade routes through land and created alternative trade routes through sea.

Another important constraint was usage of technologies derived from the colonial period. Transport specifications and technologies were different in countries like Britain and France. These two countries had their colonies in South and Southeast Asian region. This led to the presence of difference/gaps in transport infrastructure in place. Furthermore, difference in technologies created gaps in operational modalities as well. Transport systems including rail and road have different operational mechanism in India and Southeast Asia. For a long period of time, these gaps are in place and create incompatibility of systems to become integrated with each other. One of the reasons that prevented the unification of technology was rivalry among the colonial powers. The incompatible infrastructure and operational modules prevented seamless transportation from South Asia to Southeast Asia. Nevertheless, these incompatibility is reduced through modern operational mechanisms and models in both rail and road transport. This is discussed later in this paper.

The outcome of colonial period was not only differences created in infrastructure and its operational models but also strategic gaps that were laid down between countries. During the post-colonial period, countries in South and Southeast Asia became rivals on political lines. Strategic differences also prevented in establishing land transport between countries in the two regions. Pakistan, India and Bangladesh were once a single entity and became independent sovereign units during the post-colonial period. Transport with difficult terrain and with geographical constraints was seamless during the colonial period. Creation of new political boundaries compelled transport between countries happening with several breaks at border points.

As stated earlier, India's 'Look East Policy' has transformed to 'Act East Policy'. During the 25th anniversary of ASEAN-India dialogue, leaders of India and ASEAN nations reaffirmed their commitments to strengthen physical connectivity from India to Southeast Asia in line with the MPAC, 2025 and the AIM, 2020 (PIB, 2018). [9] Earlier an Action Plan (2016-2020) drafted to implement the India-ASEAN partnership included development of road routes between India and Southeast Asia particularly India-Myanmar and Thailand (IMT) trilateral highway. [10] The joint statement of ASEAN-India commemorative summit also included affirmation from countries for early implementation of the IMT trilateral highways and its extension to Cambodia, Lao PDR and Vietnam. [11]

Another important initiative is the Bay of Bengal Initiative for Multi-sectoral Technical and Economic Cooperation (BIMSTEC) through which connectivity facilitation remains an important goal for member countries of BIMSTEC. Member countries include Myanmar and Thailand also. Any progress towards operationalising seamless transport among BIMSTEC countries will help in achieving goals towards transport facilitation between South Asia and Southeast Asia.

India's endeavour to get physically integrated with ASEAN countries through land routes has two major aspects viz. (i) development of physical infrastructure and (ii) harmonization of rules for plying vehicles through countries. Development of physical infrastructure further needs development of roads and rail in India's North-East region which is considered as a gateway to Southeast Asia. Some important connectivity projects have been envisaged to strengthen connectivity between South and Southeast Asia.

Rail Connectivity

As stated earlier, an idea was coined to establish rail connectivity from New Delhi to Hanoi in 2003. The idea was further advocated at various forums including the Greater Mekong-Ganga Cooperation process. [12] The proposal of establishing rail link from New Delhi passing through countries like Myanmar, Thailand and Cambodia up to Hanoi in Vietnam was also advocated by ESCAP's proposal of Trans Asian Railway network connecting South Asia with Southeast Asia. However, establishing rail transport linkages with countries like Myanmar requires not only development of new rail infrastructure in India's North-East India but also in some parts of Myanmar. In addition to the missing links, there are differences in operational and technical standards of railways. These differences are major obstacles in realizing the dream of seamless rail connectivity across South and Southeast Asia. Rail transportation from one country to another country needs at least a robust infrastructure in place.

There is no direct connectivity between railways in India and railways in Myanmar. In case of India, rail infrastructure is in place up to Jibiram in Manipur. There was a proposal to develop new line from Jibiram to Tupul (98 km). [13] On the other hand, from Silchar to Jibiram, rail line is proposed for gauge conversion. A new line connecting Moreh in Manipur and Imphal is also under consideration. In view of the proposed rail link to Imphal, it is recommended that the construction of Moreh-Imphal line should be extended up to Mandalay in Myanmar. However, connectivity of Moreh and Imphal with Indian Railways is a project still far from reality.

It is important to note that development of railway tracks needs much attention in Southeast Asian countries particularly in countries like Myanmar, Cambodia and Lao PDR. As per one estimate, missing links in inter-country railways in Southeast Asia is as high as 38 percent of the total missing links in Trans Asian Railways networks (ESCAP, 2017). [14] Close cooperation and coordination is essential to develop the missing links in both India and the ASEAN countries.

In addition, countries in South and Southeast Asia need financial support to develop these missing links. Another important hurdle to develop missing railway links is the high cost associated with it. As per the report published by ESCAP, developmental cost of missing links of 4,763 kms. of railways in the ASEAN region is likely to be US$ 49,580 million. This also includes Yunnan province of China bordering some of the ASEAN countries like Myanmar, Lao PDR and Vietnam. Similarly, the cost of development of missing links of 2,495 kms. of railways in South Asia is likely to be US$ 9,000 million (ESCAP, 2017). [15]

Moreover, there are many projects in these countries which are under implementation but delayed or stalled owing to various reasons including technical and financial issues. For example, construction of rail infrastructure between Cambodia and Thailand has been delayed due to delay in compensation to people living along the rail line in Poipet in Cambodia (ESCAP, 2017). [16]

Such delay in the implementation of railway projects multiply the cost of development creating further apprehensions for developing large railway projects. Therefore, commercial viability of rail linkages from India to Myanmar and further to Southeast Asian countries is a matter of serious concern. It may be, therefore, noted that such a deal is not cost effective. It would be important to focus on alternative ones. And road transport is a viable alternative. In the next section, the proposed development plans in the road sector are discussed.

Road Connectivity

As part of developing internal connectivity, Government of India intends to take up road projects such as the Imphal-Moreh road project with loan assistance from ADB under its SASEC Road Connectivity Investment Programme which was approved by the Cabinet. [17] It may be noted that this road is an integral part of the trilateral highway and also part of the Asian Highway. The road directly provides connectivity with Myanmar.

Furthermore, Government of India with the objective to expedite connectivity through Myanmar established a dedicated agency which is National Highway and Infrastructure Development Corporation Ltd. (NHIDCL). [18] NHIDCL is the implementing agency for majority of projects in the North-East particularly those projects which facilitate connectivity with the neighbouring countries. NHIDCL is also an implementing agency for the Imphal-Moreh road project. [19]

As per the status available for this road project, the financial bids for the construction were received and opened in March 2018. It is expected that the construction of the road will start soon. As per the information available at the NHIDCL website, some of the other routes taken up by the Government of India for construction are listed below.

- Maram-Paren-Dimapur road.
- Kohima-Kadema-Karong-Imphal section of NH 39.
- Ukhrul-Tolloi-Tadubi in Manipur.
- 4 laning of Imphal-Moirang, NH-150 in Manipur.
- Jiribam and Tipaimukh road in Manipur.
- Lawgtlain on NH 54 to R. Zocha on Indo-Myanmar border in Mizoram.

IMT Trilateral Highway and Kaldadan Multimodal Project

IMT trilateral highway starts from India passing through

Myanmar and reaches up to Bangkok in Thailand. This route connects major business cities in Myanmar with Thailand and India. The route length is approximately 1,360 kms. [20] Construction of IMT trilateral highway has already been started with India and Thailand financing routes in Myanmar. India has already completed trilateral route from Tamu to Kalemyo via Kalewa in Myanmar which has a length of 160 kms. The segment also requires rehabilitation of 69 bridges which are in bad condition and not feasible for plying of heavy goods vehicles. Some of the sections of trilateral highway in Myanmar have a challenging terrain falling in high mountainous region.

Mountainous terrain is a major challenge for construction of the routes particularly in Kalewa-Yargi section falling in Myanmar. Parts of the trilateral highway from Myawaddy to Mae Sot are already completed by Thailand in Myanmar.

In addition to the IMT trilateral highway, India and Myanmar are developing a bilateral multimodal route involving sea, river and road. The project is known as Kaladan Multi-Modal Transit Transport Project named after Kaladan river in Myanmar which is a key inland water route. The project aims at establishing transport route from the Indian sea ports with direct sailing to Sittwe port in Myanmar. The port is connected with Kaladan river and therefore inland water transport is an important component to be developed. 158 kms from Sittwe to Paletwa in Myanmar is part of the inland water transport. A road is envisaged to provide connectivity with the river port at Paletwa from where 109 kms. of road will be upgraded to provide connectivity with India through Zorinpui border in Myanmar with North-East India. The project is expected to completed by 2019. [21]

These two projects are strategically important for India. Kaladan project is proving to be an alternate sea cum river route to reach India's North-East region. It is an alternate to Bangladesh to reach out North-East India. Operationalising Kaladan routes will require multiple transport systems and operators whereas IMT trilateral highway needs only road transport operators. IMT trilateral highway will be easy to handle when compared with the Kaladan route.

Extension of Trilateral Highway to other ASEAN Countries

At the recent India-ASEAN commemorative summit, India and member countries of ASEAN showed interest in the extension of trilateral highway to other member countries. Extension of trilateral highway to Cambodia and Vietnam as well as Lao PDR has long been discussed on different occasions. The possible extension of IMT routes in Southeast Asian countries is aimed at getting access to the markets of these countries (Basu, 2016). [22] Extension of the routes is likely to follow an international connectivity route identified under the Asian Highway. [23] It is expected that the extension of IMT trilateral highway would cover routes which connect Lao PDR with other countries in Southeast Asia like Myanmar and Thailand. Connectivity from Lao PDR can further be extended up to Hanoi in Vietnam. Therefore, there are many possible connecting highways from Myanmar to Vietnam through Lao PDR. Lao PDR and Myanmar have already established road connectivity through Friendship Bridge over the Mekong River. The Friendship Bridge was officially opened in 2015.

IMT trilateral highway has its route connectivity up to Thailand. The possible extension from Thailand is to connect with Lao PDR and Vietnam through Cambodia. As per the Asian Highway network, the following are the possible international routes in Cambodia:

- Asian Highway 11: Phnom Penh-(Cambodia)-Pakse-Vientiane (Lao PDR).
- Asian Highway 1:-Phnom Penh (Cambodia)-Ho Chi Minh City-Hanoi (Vietnam)
- Asian Highway 1: Phnom Penh-Poipet (Cambodia)-Bangkok (Thailand).
- National Road from Sre Ambel-(Cambodia) to Bangkok via Tarat (Thailand).

It is noted that Phnom Penh in Cambodia has direct road connectivity with Bangkok in Thailand. Route infrastructure in Thailand has good standards. Vietnam has also direct port access in the Pacific Ocean. Connectivity from these ports will provide alternate routes to countries like Lao PDR and Cambodia. Vietnam has direct border connectivity with Lao PDR and Cambodia. Routes connecting from Lao PDR connecting to Vietnam's ports will benefit Lao PDR as well as Vietnam. Similarly, extension of road routes from Cambodia to Ho Chin Minh is likely to open more economic opportunities for the region.

Thus, there are two possible routes in Vietnam viz. (a) connectivity from Hanoi to Lao PDR through Asian Highway 13 and (b) connectivity from Ho Chinh Mihn to Phnom Penh (Cambodia) through Asian Highway 1. On the Southern side of Thailand, the route has the potential to be extended up to Malaysia through Asian Highway 2. It may be noted that transport infrastructure is already in place but there is a need for legal framework under which vehicles from one country to other country will ply on routes identified in other countries. The next section discusses such operational models and frameworks.

Development in Operationalising India-ASEAN Road Transport Routes

Presence of physical infrastructure further needs agreed norms and rules by countries to ply their vehicles seamlessly on roads in other member countries. Notably, countries have different rules and norms for plying of vehicles on their roads in South and Southeast Asia. It is essential for countries to agree upon several technical aspects including minimum permissible weight, driving norms, visa related issues for drivers and crews, etc. Owing to differences in operational differences and lack of inter-country legal framework for the seamless movement of vehicles across borders, the logistics cost is very high implying that trade cost is also high.

At the global level, it is estimated that the cost of logistics account for 12 percent of the global GDP (ESCAP, 2017). [24] This cost for India and Southeast Asia would be higher than the global cost. This simply means higher the differences and bottlenecks for seamless transport operation higher will be the logistics cost and in turn higher will be the trade cost. High trade cost has direct implications for consumers. Therefore, cooperation and integration of transport infrastructure and services has the potential to benefit people directly.

A motor vehicle agreement (MVA) was proposed among India, Myanmar and Thailand (IMT). This agreement aimed to provide legal framework for operation of vehicles from one country to another country. Such agreements have features of providing minimum standard formulation for plying of vehicles between the countries which include provisions related to minimum agreed weights, visa and insurance, etc. These are essential parts of seamless transport connectivity. IMT MVA has implications on the future strategies of India and ASEAN with regards to the physical integration process.

Negotiations on IMT MVA started in 2015. However, the agreement is yet to be finalized and signed for implementation. [25] In order to understand the complexity of inter-country transport operation, a trial run of passenger vehicles was carried out during December 2015. Vehicles from India travelled on Imphal-Mandalay-Bagan-Naypitaw route and vehicles from Myanmar travelled on the same route from Naypitaw to Imphal and back. An IMT Friendship Motor Car Rally was also conducted in 2016 in order to sensitize the stakeholders of the Agreement. [26] During this rally, vehicles from India plied on the route that is covered under the IMT trilateral highway. The rally started from New Delhi and ended up in Bangkok. The success of this rally indicates that the existing routes connecting South and Southeast Asia have the potential to be materialized and get operationalised.

Recently, member countries of BIMSTEC also proposed a motor vehicle agreement with the objective to facilitate inter-country seamless transportation of vehicles. If materialized, BIMSTEC MVA will be an effective mechanism. Moreover, there are international mechanisms like TIR system under the International Road Transport Union (IRU) which can effectively assist regional motor vehicle agreements. India has already acceded TIR system and is implementing it. If other countries in Southeast Asia accede to this mechanism, then there will be an effective customs controlling system for international goods transportation through road routes from South Asia to Southeast Asia.

There is no direct bilateral agreement between India and Myanmar for transport operations between the two countries. On the other hand, countries in Southeast Asia like Cambodia, the Lao PDR, Thailand and Vietnam have both bilateral and regional frameworks enabling inter-country transport. Vehicles from Thailand can travel up to Vietnam through Lao PDR without any transhipment involved at border points through friendship bridges. These countries have also standardized their visa related norms and allow drivers and crews for multiple entries and exits through their territory. Entry of vehicles from one country to the other is solved through provision of issuing of temporary importation of vehicles.

Thus, India's outreach in these countries needs extension of such agreements. These countries have also agreed on permissible weights of vehicles that suit their transport infrastructure. IMT MVA can also take lessons from the issues faced by Thailand and Lao PDR while exchanging the traffic rights and allowing vehicles with goods and people.

Conclusions

There are several challenges to India's efforts to establish inter-country seamless transport linkages with Southeast Asian countries. These challenges include both infrastructural and regulatory constraints. Infrastructural constraints have already been outlined and discussed. In addition, India's development plans in respect of land transport have also been discussed earlier. It is suggested that India and ASEAN countries should establish an institutional framework which can monitor development projects in this region essential for seamless connectivity. The institutional framework should not only aim at monitoring progress of transport projects but it should also cover financing related aspects of such projects. In fact, financing is an important issue faced by all the countries in South and Southeast Asia.

India and ASEAN have already signed the free trade agreement. Such agreement implies free movement of goods with preferential treatment. However, due to lack of seamless transport mechanism, the benefits of such agreements have not materialized yet fully. Countries like India, Myanmar, Thailand and others need to agree upon a harmonized regulatory framework which should also include transport services related agreements. It has already been outlined that India, Myanmar and Thailand are negotiating a MVA for regulation of the inter-country transport. In addition, these countries are also planning to negotiate MVA under the ambit of BIMSTEC. These agreements are negotiated at regional and sub-regional levels creating a new economic block. Moreover, Myanmar, Cambodia, Thailand, Vietnam and Lao PDR are part of ASEAN and also GMS Cross Border Transport Agreement. Therefore, while negotiating such agreements, it is important to take note of the overlapping provisions.

Countries should adopt efficient practices of inter-country transport facilitation. In fact, inefficient practices coupled with absence of hard and soft infrastructure are causing transhipment at border points leading to high costs of trade. In order to address such efficiency adaptation of transport facilitation systems one must include provisions for smooth operations and less cumbersome documentation.

Digitization of operational process of transport services is an important aspect for efficient transport facilitation. Countries in South and Southeast Asia can also adopt international conventions like TIR systems. Notably, India has already acceded to the TIR convention in 2017.

In case of rail transport, developmental cost is high for countries like Myanmar, Lao PDR and Cambodia. For India, development of missing link of railways in Manipur is the foremost step to be taken for any kind of rail linkages with Myanmar and further down to Southeast Asia. However, when it comes to making choices for developing road or rail network, it is suggested that India should develop road linkages in the first phase so as to materialize the potential of trade between India and the ASEAN countries.

Finally, India and ASEAN countries are also looking for extension of IMT trilateral highway up to Vietnam through Cambodia and Thailand. Such extension only needs institutional and regulatory framework to agree upon. Because, infrastructure needed for this extension is already in place. However, this infrastructure needs strengthening at some specific routes. Of course, if countries agree, inter-country transport or movement of vehicles is possible. In fact, this is already happening between Thailand and Lao PDR and Thailand and Cambodia. India needs to negotiate with these countries at the sub-regional level to expand IMT MVA. Thus, India should aim at expansion of not only the trilateral highway but also expansion of under-negotiation IMT MVA and bringing other countries of ASEAN under the purview of the MVA.

Endnotes

1. Osius, T. And Mohan, R.C. (2013), "Enhancing India-ASEAN Connectivity", Rowman and Littlefield.
2. De, P. (2010), "ASEAN-India Connectivity: An Indian Perspective", ASEAN-India Connectivity: The Comprehensive Asia Development Plan, Phase II, ERIA Research Project Report, 7, pp. 95-150.
3. Hong, Z. (2007), "India and China: Rivals or Partners in Southeast Asia?", *Contemporary Southeast Asia*, pp. 121-142.
4. Sikri, R. (2009), "India's Look East Policy", *Asia-Pacific Review*, 16(1), pp. 131-145.
5. MEA (2003), "Race with China on Hanoi Train", Media Centre, MEA, September 5, available at:

http://www.mea.gov.in/articles-in-indian-media.htm?dtl/13205/Race+with+China+on+Hanoi+train.

6. Htun, K.W., Lwin, N.N., Naing, T.H. and Tun, K. (2011), "ASEAN-India Connectivity: A Myanmar Perspective", ASEAN-India Connectivity: The Comprehensive Asia Development Plan, Phase II.
7. De, P. (2010), "ASEAN-India Connectivity: An Indian Perspective", ASEAN-India Connectivity: The Comprehensive Asia Development Plan, Phase II, ERIA Research Project Report, 7, pp. 95-150.
8. ESCAP (2016), "Intergovernmental Agreement on the Asian Highway Network", available at: https://www.unescap.org/resources/intergovernmental-agreement-asian-highway-network.
9. PIB (2018), "Delhi Declaration of the ASEAN-India Commemorative Summit to mark the 25th Anniversary of ASEAN-India Dialogue Relations", January 25, available at: http://pib.nic.in/newsite/PrintRelease.aspx?relid=175908.
10. Ibid.
11. Ibid.
12. In Rajya Sabha during the winter session, 2003, the Foreign Affairs Minister stated, "During the Mekong-Ganga Cooperation (MGC) Ministerial Meeting in Phnom Penh in June 2003, the member countries, namely, India, Myanmar, Thailand, Lao PDR, Cambodia and Vietnam, agreed to the desirability of a rail link from New Delhi to Hanoi. Rail networks exist in India, Myanmar, Thailand, Cambodia and Vietnam, but there are missing links that would need to be laid to complete the New Delhi-Hanoi rail link".
13. AITD, National Transport Development Policy Committee, Working Group Report on Transport Network in Northeast India, Recommendations, 2012.
14. ESCAP (2017), "Review of Developments in Transport in Asia and the Pacific", United Nations Publication, Bangkok, Thailand.
15. Ibid.
16. Ibdi.
17. PIB (2017), "Under Tranche II of SASEC Road Connectivity Investment Programme of ADB", available at: http://pib.nic.in/newsite/PrintRelease.aspx?relid=167351.

18. Visit NHIDCL website
19. Current Status is available at: https://nhidcl.com/wp-content/uploads/2018/07/Manipur.pdf.
20. For more information, see notification by PIB on December 27, 2016, Year-end Review of Ministry of Road Transport and Highways, Government of India, available at: http://pib.nic.in/newsite/PrintRelease.aspx?relid=155892.
21. Please see the reply by the Minister of State in the Ministry of External Affairs in the Parliament on April 12, 2017 on question posed on Kaladan Multimodal Project, available at: http://mea.gov.in/lok-sabha.htm?dtl/28382/QUESTION_NO6280_KALADAN_MULTIMODAL_TRANSIT_TRANSPORT.
22. Basu, N. (2016), "Government Looking at Extending IMT Trilateral Highway", *The Hindu Business Line*, July 27.
23. Please see route map of Asian Highway at UNESCAP's website, available at: https://www.unescap.org/resources/asian-highway-route-map.
24. ESCAP (2017), "Review of Developments in Transport in Asia and the Pacific", United Nations Publication, Bangkok, Thailand.
25. Please see year end report 2016, of Ministry of Road Transport and Highways, published by PIB, available at: http://pib.nic.in/newsite/PrintRelease.aspx?relid=155892.
26. Ibid.

References

AITD (2012), National Transport Development Policy Committee, Working Group Report on Transport Network in Northeast India, Recommendations.

Basu, N. (2016), "Government Looking at Extending IMT Trilateral Highway", *The Hindu Business Line*, July 27.

De, P. (2010), "ASEAN-India Connectivity: An Indian Perspective", ASEAN-India Connectivity: The Comprehensive Asia Development Plan, Phase II, ERIA Research Project Report, 7, pp. 95-150.

ESCAP (2016), "Intergovernmental Agreement on the Asian Highway Network", available at: https://www.unescap.org/resources/intergovernmental-agreement-asian-highway-network.

ESCAP (2017), "Review of Developments in Transport in Asia and the Pacific", United Nations Publication, Bangkok, Thailand.

Hong, Z. (2007), "India and China: Rivals or Partners in Southeast Asia?", *Contemporary Southeast Asia*, pp. 121-142.

Htun, K.W., Lwin, N.N., Naing, T.H. and Tun, K. (2011), "ASEAN-India Connectivity: A Myanmar Perspective", ASEAN-India Connectivity: The Comprehensive Asia Development Plan, Phase II.

MEA (2003), "Race with China on Hanoi Train", Media Centre, MEA, September 5, available at: http://www.mea.gov.in/articles-in-indian-media.htm?dtl/13205/Race+with+China+on+Hanoi+train.

Osius, T. and Mohan, R.C. (2013), "Enhancing India-ASEAN Connectivity", Rowman and Littlefield.

PIB (2018), "Delhi Declaration of the ASEAN-India Commemorative Summit to mark the 25th Anniversary of ASEAN-India Dialogue Relations", January 25, available at: http://pib.nic.in/newsite/PrintRelease.aspx?relid=175908.

PIB (2017), "Under Tranche II of SASEC Road Connectivity Investment Programme of ADB", July 12, available at: http://pib.nic.in/newsite/PrintRelease.aspx?relid=167351.

Sikri, R. (2009), "India's Look East Policy", *Asia-Pacific Review*, 16(1), pp. 131-145.

8

Geo-economics of India's Engagements with Cambodia, Laos, Myanmar and Vietnam (CLMV)

Faisal Ahmed and Farhan Alam

Abstract

India and the countries of CLMV which includes Cambodia, Laos, Myanmar and Vietnam share deep historical ties. Their contemporary relations too have been quiet engaging and friendly not only in terms of trade but also in cultural aspects. Moreover, India has engaged with these countries both at the bilateral level as well as with the CLMV congregation as a whole. In this paper, we identify six enablers viz. defence and security cooperation, exclusive economic zones, global value chains, cyber security, small and medium enterprises, and services sector which can further deepen India's engagements with the CLMV, amid changing geopolitical architecture and politico-economic alignments in the Indo-Pacific region. This chapter deciphers the geo-economic of India-CLMV engagements and argues that with more policy space to the enablers, further mutual advantages in economic and cultural spheres can be leveraged.

Introduction

The congregation of four countries of the Association of Southeast Asian Nations (ASEAN) viz. Cambodia, Laos, Myanmar and Vietnam popularly known as CLMV in policy and academic discourse, was formed to enhance mutual cooperation. ASEAN is considered as the most advanced regional cooperation effort after the European Union (EU) in terms of general cooperation between members. [1] With the integration of Cambodia, Laos, Myanmar and Vietnam into ASEAN in the 1990s, ASEAN's geo-economic gravity has escalated manifold. Security and economic concerns were the major reason behind this integration. There was also a need to strengthen ASEAN's diplomatic position at multilateral level (Soja, 2017). For the development of socio-cultural and economic communities, it is imperative for CLMV countries to enhance their cooperation (Yoshimatsu, 2010).

The development of East Asia has much to do with the development of the Mekong region. The East Asian market liberalization is highly dependent on level of integration of ASEAN including that within the CLMV and their socio-economic development (Yoshimatsu, 2010). Japan has increased its economic assistance to CLMV in order to improve its geo-strategic base in the Indo-Pacific region. Through these regional cooperation initiatives, Japan is also playing a key role in the region. Sudo (2009) mentioned that it has extended development assistance to ASEAN countries, including CLMV. Also, owing to the integration efforts at the ASEAN level, the trade ratio is increasing within CLMV with 72.6 percent of the tariff lines being duty free in 2014 (Cuyvers et al., 2017).

Since India and CLMV have deep historical and civilizational ties, it is imperative that their contemporary relationship be studied in various perspectives. In the emerging global order, the concept of India-CLMV geo-economics should therefore also be analyzed through the lens of the Indo-Pacific region. The concept of Free and Open Indo-Pacific, which is in itself a geo-economic ideation of regional architecture in Asia, Africa and Oceania, is re-defining the political and economic realignments. President Donald Trump has described this term as "a place where sovereign and independent nations, with diverse cultures and many different dreams, can all prosper side-by-side, and thrive in freedom and peace". [2]

As the significance of the Indo-Pacific region increases, it becomes imperative to assess the role of India, China, US, as well as the ASEAN countries. Therefore, CLMV which makes up the developing economies in ASEAN too have a role to play in the re-definition of the regional architecture. In the Indo-Pacific architecture, Vietnam is the most important country among the CLMV. The issues of South China Sea are primarily a concern for Vietnam and other stakeholders including India. A study by Scott (2013) discussed India's strategic approach in South China Sea. Also, Ahmed (2012) has examined the role of United Nations Convention on Law of the Sea (UNCLOS) related to navigation, transit regimes, EEZ issues and the like.

In fact, there are only few academic studies about India's engagements in the Indo-Pacific context. For instance, studies like Chacko (2012) and Das (2013) discussed about India's defence-related agreements with ASEAN and India's regional vision in the Indo-Pacific respectively. Another study by Prasad (2017) has discussed the role of India and Japan in the Indo-Pacific. Pant (2018) has discussed about the strategic relationship between India and Vietnam. In fact, India and Vietnam have deepened their relationship to a great extent. A bilateral meeting was held between Prime Minister Narendra Modi and the Vietnamese President Tran Dai Quang in New Delhi in early 2018 in which the two countries decided to further collaborate on defence and security cooperation, and to establish a rule-based security architecture in the Indo-Pacific region. [3]

Interestingly, other studies by Garge (2016) and Lee and Lee (2016) discussed Japan-India cooperation and security cooperation in the context of the Indo-Pacific region. Also, in April 2018, the Defence Minister of Vietnam visited Japan to discuss security and strategic alignment issues pertinent to the Indo-Pacific region. [4]

Again, there are issues like Belt and Road Initiatives (Esteban, 2018), ASEAN's centrality in Australia's Indo-Pacific outlook (Ha, 2018), and India's strategic approach toward ASEAN and the Indo-Pacific (Bajpaee, 2017; Garge, 2017) which are of immense importance in discourse.

As far as India's trade and security engagements with ASEAN and other mega-trade blocks like Regional Comprehensive Economic Partnership (RCEP) etc. are concerned, there are several academic studies by scholars like Alam (2015), Collin (2013), Raghurampatruni (2012), Vu and Asher (2009) etc. Also, there is enough literature on Asia-Pacific economic integration both as a region as well as from a country's perspective. These include Hidayat (2013), Wignaraja (2015), Mathur et al. (2016), Das et al. (2016), and Gantz (2016).

The present paper therefore discusses India's relations with the CLMV countries in the context of Indo-Pacific as well. The subsequent sections of this paper examine the trade portfolio, based on analysis of trade statistics both from country-wise as well as commodity-wise angle. Further, this paper identifies and analyses six key enablers of India's geo-economic engagements with the CLMV countries.

India-CLMV Trade Relations

CLMV has a geographical proximity to India, which entails India to enhance its geo-economic and geo-political cooperation with these countries and the region. Owing to the different trade routes passing through ASEAN, this region acquires immense importance for India's trade. The Government of India has approved a Project Development Fund (PDF) for CLMV. This PDF will be monitored under the chairmanship of the Commerce Secretary. The industrial sector will benefit through it.

Moreover, it will boost the value chain and production networks in the Indo-Pacific region. The 5th India-CLMV Business Conclave was held in Phnom Penh, Cambodia in May 2018. It was jointly organized by the Ministry of Commerce and Industry, Government of India in collaboration with the Ministry of Commerce, Government of Cambodia. It aims to enhance the regional consolidation and creation of value chain among India and the CLMV countries. The key areas of cooperation include small and medium enterprises (SMEs), manufacturing, agriculture, fisheries, plantation, healthcare, education, information technology and skill development. The conclave also discussed bilateral trade between India and Cambodia, Vietnam and Laos.

In fact, India and Vietnam have largely been able to leverage their civilizational connect into developing contemporary relations. The two countries have now developed robust institutional and policy frameworks. Also, there are academic studies which have discussed issues related to India-Vietnam trade relations. For instance, Nguyen et al. (2016) has compared the levels of efficiency, innovation and competition in the economies of India, China and Vietnam. In January 2018, the Vietnamese Ambassador to India, Ton Sinh Thanh rightly remarked, "India plays a leading role in the Indian Ocean region, while Vietnam holds an important geopolitical position in the Pacific region". [5] Also, in 2016, both countries upgraded their Strategic Partnership (2007-2017) into a Comprehensive Strategic Partnership.

The trade relation between India and the CLMV countries has been evolving and has witnessed an increasing trend. In a decade, India's exports to Cambodia increased from US$ 53.85 million in 2008 to US$ 120.17 million in 2017 (Figure 8.1). Overall, India's total exports to CLMV increased from US$ 2.1 billion in 2008 to US$ 9.32 billion in 2017.

India's imports from CLMV also witnessed a positive growth trend in a decade. For instance, India's imports from Laos increased from US$ 0.52 million in 2008 to US$ 248.63 million in 2017 (Figure 8.2). India's imports from the CLMV congregation have increased four-fold in a decade. In 2008, India's total imports from CLMV were pegged at US$ 1,282.66 million, which increased to US$5,183.66 million in 2017.

The commodity-wise analysis of major Indian exports to CLMV reveals insightful statistics. When taken at 2-digit HS Code, the top 7 export commodities (in terms of value as in 2017) have been identified in Table 8.1.

These commodities constitute a major chunk of the total trade between the two countries.

Figure 8.1: India's Exports to CLMV Countries (2008-17)

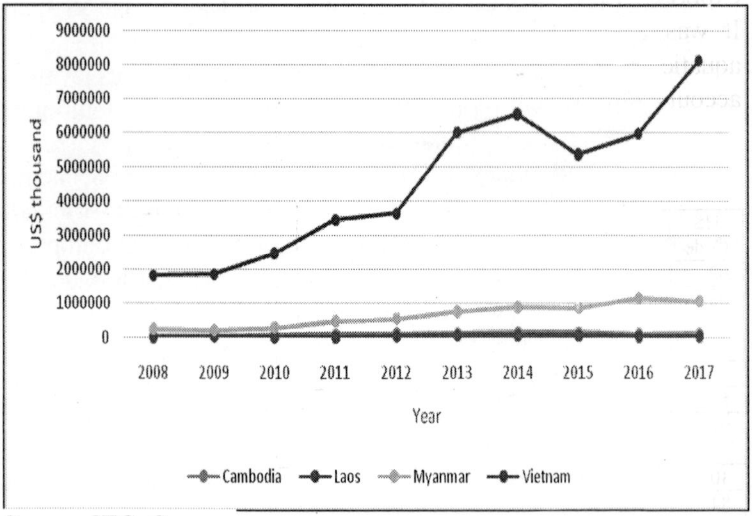

Source: ITC, Geneva.

Figure 8.2: India's Imports from CLMV countries (2008-17)

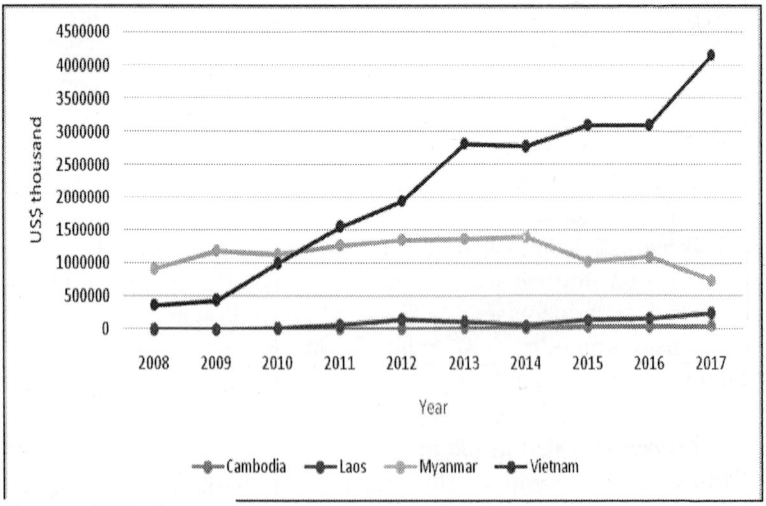

Source: ITC, Geneva.

Meat and edible meat offal (HS Code 02) is India's major export to CLMV and accounted for US$ 2366.05 million in 2017. It was followed by fish and crustaceans, molluscs and other aquatic invertebrates (classified under HS Code 03) which accounted for US$ 1809.94 million (Table 8.1).

Table 8.1: India's Top 7 Exports to CLMV

(US$ thousand)

HS Code	Commodities	2010	2011	2012	2013
02	Meat and edible meat offal	3,12,654	7,33,398	8,43,824	1,93,6362
03	Fish and crustaceans, molluscs and other aquatic invertebrates	1,08,348	5,10,222	4,77,824	10,11,294
72	Iron and steel	44,029	1,04,031	1,25,000	4,92,986
52	Cotton	1,88,789	1,34,064	1,94,422	4,12,783
09	Coffee, tea, maté and spices	19,983	43,580	1,26,370	1,93,990
30	Pharmaceutical products	1,73,190	2,23,982	2,66,018	3,42,232
84	Machinery, mechanical appliances, nuclear reactors, boilers; parts thereof	1,33,609	1,81,413	1,45,673	2,28,196

contd...

HS Code	Commodities	2014	2015	2016	2017
02	Meat and edible meat offal	2337714	1970836	1913039	2366053
03	Fish and crustaceans, molluscs and other aquatic invertebrates	1099066	933861	1264853	1809942
72	Iron and steel	216128	111237	256724	944241
52	Cotton	544712	355992	299641	450603
09	Coffee, tea, maté and spices	220878	210300	280467	415909
30	Pharmaceutical products	364299	349952	345519	360025
84	Machinery, mechanical appliances, nuclear reactors, boilers; parts thereof	342960	255413	265262	311130

Source: ITC, Geneva.

Moreover, Table 8.2 reveals that India's topmost imports from CLMV include commodities which come under HS Code 85 and accounted for US$ 1216.02 million in 2017. It comprises of electrical machinery and equipment and parts thereof, sound recorders and reproducers, television image and sound recorders and reproducers, and parts. This is followed by edible vegetables and certain roots and tubers thereof which is classified under HS Code 07 and accounted for US$ 5,33.09 million (Table 8.2).

Table 8.2: India's Top 7 Imports from CLMV

(US$ thousand)

HS Code	Commodities	2010	2011	2012	2013
85	Electrical machinery and equipment etc..	3,53,272	5,32,350	7,53,070	14,67,613
07	Edible vegetables and certain roots.	6,63,709	5,86,188	5,96,671	6,11,206
84	Machinery, mechanical appliances, nuclear reactors.	72,089	1,46,122	1,39,991	2,23,847
74	Copper and articles thereof	1,162	9,905	10,042	31,730
28	Inorganic chemicals; organic or inorganic compounds.	36,295	48,331	56,820	73,995
44	Wood and articles of wood; wood charcoal	4,41,061	6,27,211	7,24,171	7,91,423
09	Coffee, tea, and spices	79,116	1,04,845	1,25,360	1,30,444

contd...

HS Code	Commodities	2014	2015	2016	2017
85	Electrical machinery and equipment etc.	10,95,474	9,79,984	8,95,674	12,16,022
07	Edible vegetables and certain roots.	7,98,769	8,54,584	8,31,030	5,33,093
84	Machinery, mechanical appliances nuclear reactors.	1,94,513	3,12,308	3,40,841	4,10,041
74	Copper and articles thereof	56,887	98,156	1,70,848	3,84,445
28	Inorganic chemicals; organic or inorganic compounds.	1,11,468	1,63,873	2,24,401	2,89,761
44	Wood and articles of wood; wood charcoal	6,41,438	2,46,380	2,32,638	2,27,321
09	Coffee, tea, and spices	2,35,076	1,87,545	2,19,031	2,23,897

Source: ITC, Geneva.

Geo-economic Enablers

It is now pertinent to identify those geo-economic enablers that have the potential to strengthen relations between India and the CLMV countries. These enablers include both macro- and micro-perspectives and require enough policy attention from both the sides (Figure 8.3).

Figure 8.3: Geo-economic Enablers of India-CLMV Engagements

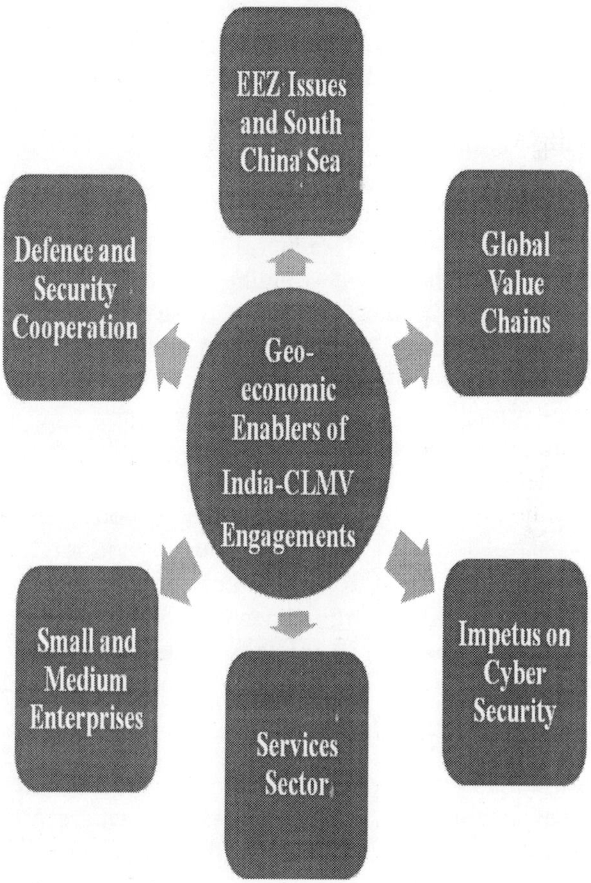

Source: Authors.

Defence and Security Co-operation: Defence and security cooperation is a key enabler to strengthen ties between India and the CLMV countries. India-Cambodia bilateral defence cooperation is also evident with annual training for Royal Cambodian Armed Forces in peacekeeping missions. Defence training programme under ITEC, and visits of Indian Navy and Indian Coast Guard has also taken place with Cambodia. On a goodwill visit, Indian Coast Guard Ship 'Samrat' visited Cambodia in November 2016. In November 2016, India also gifted 15 mine sniffer dogs to Cambodia. [6]

Moreover, India has gifted jeeps and parachutes to Laos Army in January 2003 and in April 2009. India has also imparted training to Laos Army in March 2011, and in February-March 2013.

With Myanmar, India has defence ties in the form of signing of MoU on border cooperation, training, army, air force, and navigation. In November 2016, CNS Admiral Sunil Lamba, and in May 2017, General Bipin Rawat paid a visit to Myanmar. Both held wide-ranging strategic talks with their counterpart in Myanmar to strengthen the defence ties. Sr. Gen Min Aung Hliang of Myanmar paid a visit to India in July 2017, to further strengthen the defence ties between the two countries.

Strategic partnership with Vietnam has also emerged in the form of defence cooperation with India. A MoU was signed by both the countries in November 2009, to boost strategic ties. Every year, 50 Indian Technical and Economic Cooperation (ITEC) slots are offered to Vietnamese defence personnel. The two countries are building deeper economic and geo-political engagements. They have already upgraded their bilateral Strategic Partnership (2007-17) into a Comprehensive Strategic Partnership. Military, maritime and cyber security are the key areas of cooperation.

In February 2016, Indian Navy organized International Fleet Review, at Vishakhapatnam, India, where Vietnamese ships got the participation. In July 2018, India extended a US$

500 million line of credit to Vietnam to strengthen the defence ties. Also, India and Vietnam committed for a joint co-production in defence, which also includes technology transfer from India to Vietnam. Equipment procurement and capacity building projects and initiatives are also underway in Vietnam. In fact, the ASEAN Defence Ministers Meeting (ADMM)+ is also crucial in this context. Though, India and Vietnam have struck deals related to it, ADMM is also significant in the context of India's relations with the CLMV congregation.

Exclusive Economic Zones: India has a geo-strategic presence over South China Sea, in the form of oil and natural gas exploration activities. ONGC Videsh Ltd. of India has its strong presence in the continental shelf and exclusive economic zone (EEZ) of Vietnam. China has opposed OVL's exploration activities in the Vietnam's EEZ in the South China Sea. Such geopolitical challenges in the South China Sea and the issue of exclusive economic zone (EEZ) has geo-economic implications for India as well as the CLMV. India has often expressed concern over freedom of navigation in the South China Sea. In 2016, India also supported a verdict of the Permanent Court of Arbitration of the International Court of Justice to this effect. In 2017, on the sidelines of the ASEAN summit, Prime Minister Modi held talks with Prime Minister Phucand and other leaders and stressed on deepening relations.

From 2006, OVL and GAIL are consortium partners with Daewoo in Myammar, to develop offshore blocks with state-owned Myanmar Oil and Gas Enterprise (MOGE), till the next 30 years i.e. 2036. Myanmar has hydrocarbon deposits in their EEZ, and faces confrontations from Bangladesh over the issue.

Moreover, in 2017, both Cambodia and Laos have negotiated their issues related to overlapping territorial claims in South China Sea with China. Cambodia and Laos have agreed with China over 'four-point consensuses' on South China Sea issue.

Global Value Chains: Overall, almost two-thirds of total international trade in goods happens in intermediate goods, and they are therefore a significant participant in the global value chain (GVC). The global production networks and the distribution of value chain activities are geographically dispersed across a region based on raw material availability, and labour and cost advantages. Despite the shortcomings in transportation and infrastructure sector, Cambodia has increased its share in the GVC. From September 15-17, 2015, Vice-President of India led a high level delegation to Cambodia, where he held official talks with the Cambodian Prime Minister and signed a MoU for 'Implementation of Quick Impacts Projects under Mekong-Ganga Cooperation initiatives'.

Even for Laos which is also a LDC, its participation in GVC is very dismal. Mostly, it is derived mainly from its minerals resources and garments. Also, garment value chain is a key component of Myanmar's GVC. In fact, development of GVC in CLMV and also partnership with India through frameworks like Bay of Bengal Initiative for Multi-Sectoral Technical and Economic Cooperation (BIMSTEC) (especially related to Myanmar, which is a BIMSTEC member) or Mekong-Ganga Cooperation (which includes India, Thailand and all CLMV countries) is necessary. Also, there is need to evolve the production and value chain network within CLMV countries as well. Wisuttisak and Binh (2016) argue that Thailand businesses face high business risks when entering into CLMV. For GVC, India and CLMV can collaborate in sectors like apparel, food processing, footwear, oil and gas, electronic goods, agricultural goods, etc.

Moreover, diversification of trade basket is also important to support the participation of these countries in GVC. Trade statistics as given in Tables 8.1 and 8.2 clearly reveal that most of the trade between India and CLMV happens in conventional sectors only. The trade basket needs to be diversified.

Cyber Security: Information and cyber security is now a key determinant in the evolving relationship between India and CLMV countries. For instance, a MoU was signed between

India and Vietnam in the field of cyber security in 2016 at Hanoi with the aim to augment capacity building and develop institutional capacity. Also, Cambodia is on the verge of cyber security issue, both on its internal and external fronts. Recently, in 2017, a United States cyber security firm claimed that China affected the general elections in Cambodia.

In Laos, Lao Computer Emergency Response Team (LaoCERT) is the initiative of Government of Laos to tackle the growing concern of cyber security issues in the country. It was established in the year 2012. In the year 2014, LaoCERT became a member of Asia Pacific CERT (APCERT). To improve upon the regional cyber security cooperation, LaoCERT signed a MoU with Thailand Computer Emergency Response Team (ThaiCERT) in 2013, with Indonesia Security Incidents Response Team (IDSERT) in 2015, and with Vietnam Computer Emergency Response Team (VNCERT) and China Computer Emergency Response Team (CNCERT) in 2017. Moreover, Microsoft's Security Intelligence Report of 2017 suggests that Myanmar ranks 4th among the Asia-Pacific countries that are most exposed to cyber threats. Myanmar lacks rules and regulations and protection against cyber crimes and it is being monitored and governed by an electronic transactions law. Therefore, given the expertise of India in handling cyber security issues, collaboration between India and CLMV can help build a secure cyber architecture.

Small and Medium Enterprises: The small and medium enterprises (SMEs) are integral to the growth story of developing and least developed countries alike. India and CLMV can enhance their export potential as well as their participation in the GVCs by mutually focusing on the SMEs sector.

Nearly 40-50 percent of Cambodia's population is employed with the SME sector, while its GDP growth stands at around 7 percent. The retail and wholesale sectors are major contributors of the SME sector with around 50 percent share. However, weak legal frameworks and limited access to finance are major constraints of SMEs in Cambodia.

In Laos, 97 percent of SMEs are facing larger challenges including those related to bureaucratic inefficiency, less transparency and inconsistent regulatory frameworks. Challenges are more apparent in rural parts of the country. In Myanmar, SMEs are a major driving factor as it holds 90 percent of the total businesses. According to the Department of Industrial Supervision and Inspection, Ministry of Industry, Myanmar, there are 48,778 privately owned registered SMEs. [7]

In fact, issues related to the SMEs have already gotten policy attention in all the regional agreements including ASEAN, MGC, BIMSTEC and SAARC and also mega-blocks like the Comprehensive and Progressive Trans-Pacific Partnership (CP-TPP) and Regional Comprehensive Economic Partnership (RCEP). With India's 'Look East Policy' and now its successor 'Act East Policy', there is enough scope to leverage the trade and economic benefits through SME cluster development. For SME development, India and CLMV need to address challenges related to supply-side constraints, innovation, financing, technology, innovations and sustainability issues.

Services Sector: An important enabler is potentially the services sector which can help boost cooperation between India and the CLMV countries. India's global exports of services was US$ 161.8 billion as of 2016, while CLMV's global services exports was relatively very low. The services sector of Cambodia accounts for 35.9 percent of country's GDP. Tourism and real estate sectors are the major contributors in services sector. Cambodia, in fact, needs FDI in services to boost its economy. [8] Also, Laos is witnessing a decline in its services sector, which stands at 4.6 percent, which is lower than the target of 9 percent. [9] Services sector representation in national GDP is also falling. Myanmar is a growing economy in ASEAN, and has a lot of opportunities for services sector development. The healthcare and education sectors are the major contributors in Myanmar's service sector. Service sector contributes 38 percent of Myanmar's total GDP.

The cooperation between India and CLMV in financial

services, education, healthcare, audio-visual services, tourism, and ICT will provide meaningful output in terms of job creation in these economies.

Conclusion

We have identified six enablers viz. defence and security cooperation, exclusive economic zones, global value chains, cyber security, small and medium enterprises, and services sector, which solicit enough policy space by India and CLMV countries. Besides this, there is a need to further liberalise Mode-4, and work towards people-to-people contact and other confidence building measures. All such enablers and initiatives will further deepen India's relations with ASEAN in general and CLMV countries in particular. These geo-economic enablers shall help leverage mutual advantages in economic and cultural spheres.

Endnotes

1. E. Hörhager (2016), "The EU Pivot towards Southeast Asia: Between Regional Integration and Security Dynamics", in: J. Van Der Harts, T. Halbertsam (eds.), 'China, East Asia and the European Union: Strong Economics, Weak Politics?', Brill, 2016, p. 218.
2. Asia Maritime Transparency Initiative, CSIS, available at: https://amti.csis.org/making-foip-appealing-southeast-asia.
3. "India, Vietnam to Work Jointly for Free, Open Indo-Pacific", *The Indian Express*, March 4, 2018.
4. "Japan-Vietnam Defence Relations in the Indo-Pacific Spotlight", Prashanth Parameswaran, The Diplomat, April 11, 2018, available at: https://thediplomat.com/2018/04/japan-vietnam-defense-relations-in-the-indo-pacific-spotlight.
5. "Ambassador: Vietnam-India Ties Increasingly Important to Indo-Pacific", January 10, 2018, available at: http://en.qdnd.vn/ovs/news/ambassador-vietnam-india-ties-increasingly-important-to-indo-pacific-488707.
6. https://www.mea.gov.in/Portal/ForeignRelation/1_Cambodia_November_2017.pdf.

7. "Global New Light of Myanmar", October 25, 2017, *Business*.
8. www.jica.go.jp/cambodia/english/office/topics/c8h0vm000001o aq8-att/investment_05.pdf.
9. "Service Sector in Laos Slows but Industry Surges", *The Nation*, Thailand Portal, May 4, 2017.

References

Alam, M.I. (2015), "Indo-Asian Trade Relations: An Analysis", *Journal of International Economics*, Vol. 6, No. 1, pp. 73-106.

Bajpayee, C. (2017), "Dephasing India's Look East/Act East Policy", *Contemporary Southeast Asia*, Vol. 39, No. 2, pp. 348-372.

Brewster, D. (2013), "India's Defence Strategy and the India-ASEAN Relationship", *India Review*, Vol. 12, No. 3, pp. 151-164.

Chacko, P. (2012), "India and the Indo-Pacific: An Emerging Regional Vision", Indo-Pacific Governance Research Centre, Policy Briefs, Issue 5, November.

Chen, Juliana W. (2007), "Achieving Supreme Excellence: How China is Using Agreements with ASEAN to Overcome Obstacle of its Leadership in Asian Regional Economic Integration", *Chicago Journal of International Law,* Vol. 7, No. 2, pp. 655-674.

Chong, A. and Wu, S. (2018), "Indo-Pacific vs. Asia-Pacific: Contending Visions?", RSIS, Policy Brief No. 34, February.

Collin, K.S.L. (2013), "ASEAN Perspectives on Naval Cooperation with India: Singapore and Vietnam", *India Review*, Vol. 12, No. 3, pp. 186-206.

Cuyvers, Ludo, Steenkamp, Ermie, Viviers, Wilma, Rossouw, Riaan and Cameron, Martin (2017), "Identifying Thailand's High-potential Export Opportunities in ASEAN+3 Countries", *Journal of International Trade Law and Policy,* Vol. 16, No. 1, pp. 2-33.

Das, A.K. (2013), "India's Defence-Related Agreements with ASEAN States: A Timeline", *India Review*, Vol. 12, No. 3, pp. 130-133.

Das, R.U., Rishi, M. and Dubey, J.D. (2016), "ASEAN Plus Six and Successful FTAs: Can India Propel Intra-Industry Trade Flows?", *The Journal of Developing Areas*, Vol. 50, No. 2, pp. 40-57.

Das, Upendra Ram (2015), "India's Strategy for Economic

Integration with CLMV", Department of Commerce, Ministry of Commerce and Industry, Government of India.

Dosch, Jörn (2006), "Vietnam's ASEAN Membership Revisited: Golden Opportunity or Golden Cage?", *Contemporary Southeast Asia*, Vol. 28, No. 2, pp. 234-258.

Esteban, M. (2018), "Europe in the Face of a New Privileged Strategic Scenario: The Indo-Pacific Region", Expert Comment 15/2018-20/2/2018, Real Instituto, Elcano Royal Institute.

Garge, R. (2016), "The India-Japan Strategic Partnership: Evolving Synergy in the Indo-Pacific", *Australian Journal of Maritime and Ocean Affairs*, Vol. 8, No. 3, pp. 257-266.

Garge, R. (2017), "Maritime Outreach as Part of India's 'Act East' Policy", *Australian Journal of Maritime and Ocean Affairs*, 2017, Vol. 9, No. 3, pp. 150-167.

Gaur, Seema (2003), "Framework Agreement on Comprehensive Economic Co-operation between India and ASEAN: First Step towards Economic Integration", *Asean Economic Bulletin*, Vol. 20, No. 3, pp. 283-291.

Giang, Bui Truong and Thanh, Vo Tri (2007), "Approach to Development Gaps in ASEAN: A Vietnamese Perspective", *ASEAN Economic Bulletin*, Vol. 24, No. 1, pp. 164-180.

Grantz, D.A. (2016), "The TPP and RCEP: Mega-Trade Agreements for the Pacific Rim", *Arizona Journal of International and Comparative Law*, Vol. 33, No. 1, pp. 57-70.

Hidayat, A.S. (2013), "ASEAN-India Strategic Partnership and Design of Future Regional Trading Architecture", Economic Research Centre, Indonesian Institute of Sciences, pp. 1-13.

Hong. Zhao (2007), "India and China: Rivals or Partners in Southeast Asia?", *Contemporary Southeast Asia,* Vol. 29, No. 1, pp. 121-142.

Lee, J. and Lee, L. (2016), "Japan-India Cooperation and Abe's Democratic Security Diamond: Possibilities, Limitations and the View from Southeast Asia", *Contemporary Southeast Asia*, Vol. 38, No. 2, pp. 284-308.

Mathur, S.K., Arora, R. and Bhardwaj, M. (2016), "Relative Benefits/Losses of India Aligning with RCEP and BRICS Countries under the Conjecture of Free Trade Area in Goods", ARTNeT Working Paper Series, No. 160, pp. 1-35.

Nguyen, T.P.T., Nghiem, S.H., Roca, E. and Sharma, P. (2016),

"Efficiency, Innovation and Competition: Evidence from Vietnam, China and India", *Empirical Economics,* 51:1235-1259, Springer-Verlag Berlin Heidelberg.

Pant, H.V. (2018), "India and Vietnam: A Strategic Partnership in the Making", RSIS, Policy Brief, April.

Prasad, N. (2017), "India, Japan, and the Indo-Pacific: Breaking Out of the Middle Power Status", *Asia-Pacific Bulletin*, EastWestCenter.org/APB, No. 384, June 15.

Raghurampatruni, R. (2012), "Revealed Comparative Advantage: An Analysis for India and ASEAN", *Sona Global Management Review*, Vol. 6, No. 4.

Rasiah, Rajah, Asirvatham, James and Adamu, Ibrahim M. (2017), "Foreign Direct Investment, GDP Growth and Trade Liberalization: Evidence from Pioneering ASEAN Members", *Journal of Economic Cooperation and Development*, Vol. 38, No. 1, pp. 97-126.

Salazar, Lorraine C. and Das, Sanchita Basu (2007), "Bridging the ASEAN Developmental Divide: Challenges and Prospects", *ASEAN Economic Bulletin*, Vol. 24, No. 1, pp. 1-14.

Scott, D. (2013), "India's Role in the South China Sea: Geopolitics and Geo-economics in Play", *India Review*, Vol. 12, No. 2, pp. 51-69.

Sermcheep, Sineenat and Chirathivat, Suthiphand (2015), "Moving the AEC Beyond 2015: Managing Domestic Economic Interests in Thailand", *Journal of Southeast Asian Economies,* Vol. 32, No. 2, pp. 154-178.

Severino, Rodolfo C. (2007), "The ASIAN Developmental Divide and the Initiative for ASEAN Integration", *ASEAN Economic Bulletin,* Vol. 24, No. 21, pp. 35-44.

Soja, Pawel (2017), "Integration of the CLMV Countries with the Association of Southeast Asian Nations", *The Polish Quarterly of International Affairs*, Vol. 4, pp. 44-69.

Sudo, Sueo (2009), "Japan's ASEAN Policy: Reactive or Proactive in the Face of a Rising China in East Asia?", *Asian Perspective,* Vol. 33, No. 1, pp. 137-158.

Vu, K. and Asher, M. (2009), "India-Vietnam: A Comparative Analysis of Economic Performance", *International Journal of Business Insight and Transformation*, October 08-March 09.

Wignaraja, G. (2015), "India's Economic Potential in Looking East", *Asia Pacific Bulletin*, No. 300.

Wisuttisak, Pornchai and Binh, Nguyen Ba (2016), "The Regulatory and Commercial Environment for Franchising in Thailand in the Wake of the ASEAN Integrating Market", *IIUM Law Journal,* Vol. 24, No. 1, pp. 107-127.

Yoshimatsu, Hidetaka (2006), "Collective Action Problems and Regional Integration in ASEAN", *Contemporary Southeast Asia*, Vol. 28, No. 1, pp. 115-140.

Yoshimatsu, Hidetaka (2010), "The Mekong Region, Regional Integration, and Political Rivalry among ASEAN, China and Japan", *Asian Perspective*, Vol. 34, No. 3, pp. 71-111.

Index

Index